Civil Conversation

Book I

The rewards that can be
reaped from conversation and teaching how
to get to know good company from bad.

by
Stefano Guazzo, 1574

Translated by
George Pettie, 1581

Adapted by
David Neitz, 2021

Edited by
Helen Bowden, 2021

Dedication

To my wife Sharon who is my best friend. Thank you for supporting me as I try something new.

Introduction

You might be wondering why someone would take a 450 plus-year-old book and rewrite it. I recently retired and while spending time working on the genealogy of my family, an idea started to take form. I had discovered a treasure trove of information about one of my great…great grandfathers, Thomas Clarke. He was not famous but lived an extraordinary life that is worth writing about. He was born in 1599 and lived to the ripe old age of 98. I decided that I would write a book about his life. A tremendous amount of history occurred during his lifetime. While researching his life, I uncovered strong evidence that he had read *The Civil Conversation,* which was a popular series of books amongst the middle class in the late sixteenth and early seventeenth centuries. I am fairly certain that he applied a lot of the life lessons found in these books to his own life. With this information in hand, so I could better understand him, I ordered the books.

I have read several books from the late 16th century

and Tudor English is not for the faint of heart. It is difficult to understand and comprehend. The Tudor alphabet contains twenty-four letters, as opposed to the present-day alphabet of twenty-six letters. The letters "u" and "v" and "i" and "j" were the same and are interchangeable. Writers used a lot of odd phrases and word usage, an excessive amount of commas and semicolons, rarely would you find a paragraph break, and run-on sentences were common practice. Words were written phonetically and would sometimes be spelled differently even within the same sentence.

I purchased the Tudor Translations' version of *The Civil Conversation* which was published in 1925 with a very detailed introduction by Sir Edward Sullivan, 1852-1928, an Irish lawyer and bookbinder. I highly recommend reading his introduction because he provides some interesting insights into the author Stefano Guazzo. He includes information about the two French authors who translated the book into French and details regarding George Pettie and Bartholomew Young who translated the books into English. Sir Edward indicates that the book had a strong appeal to William Shakespeare, who most likely read it when he was seventeen years old, providing forty-plus pages of detailed analysis of how and what Shakespeare borrowed and paraphrased from the books during his career as a playwright and poet.

Stefano Guazzo, the author of *La Civil Conversatione*, was born in 1530 in Casale, the capital of Montferrat, in northern Italy. He studied law and passed away in December 1593. The books contain numerous proverbs, poems, and sayings that are effectively sprinkled throughout. It was first published in 1574 in Brescia and was very popular amongst the middle and working class of that time. Ten editions were produced with the last printing in 1621. Two French versions were also published several years after the book gained some notoriety throughout Italy. George Pettie translated the first three books into English in 1581 and in 1586 Bartholomew Young completed the translation of the fourth book.

After reading the books, I concluded that they should be shared with everyone instead of having them relegated to history to be studied and analyzed by academics. We spend so much time with our heads down, on our phones communicating through texts and tweets, that we have forgotten how to have a civil conversation with another person. The books are a very polished form of prose that follows the natural flow of speech during the sixteenth century. It was written for the common man in a simple but serious way, sophisticated without an air of arrogance, and informal without any crude or coarse language. It is full of lively figures of speech, descriptive illustrations, and a host of proverbs, poems, colloquialisms, and sayings of that time that are still in use today. The books are somewhat humorous at times and eloquent at other times. There is a religious tone in places because religion was so intertwined within their lives, but it's not over the top or in your face. There are references to Greek and Roman mythology mixed in to support the speaker's position. It is a picture of Italian life and morals, both public and domestic. It discusses the benefits and rewards that can be garnered from having conversations with others, teaching how to determine good company from bad, and how flattery affects our everyday life. The books were intended to be an account of the middle class instead of people of a higher social order.

This book is based on the English translation by George Pettie and the original Italian as a reference when I had difficulties understanding what George had written. A conscious effort was made to not alter the voices of the characters and I credit my sister-in-law Helen, who edited the book, for helping accomplish this. She was also instrumental in helping me work through the grammar issues that arose while adapting the book to modern English. Paragraphs and chapters were added to break the conversation into chunks so it could be more easily digested. This also provides an easily identifiable break in the story if you need to set the book down for a minute.

I hope, you the reader, enjoy this book as much as I do.

Table of Contents

Preface 1
Solitude 5
It is good not to be alone 13
Man was not born only for himself 23
Learning never gets old 39
Solitude can refresh the soul 51
The nature and quality of conversation 59
Avoid the Intolerable 67
Straddling a very fine line 77
Flattery, the good, the bad, and the ugly 91
The motives of ambition 119
Wrap it up 125
Letter to the Lady Norrice 135
Note from George Pettie 139
Index 147
Bibliography 151
Notes 153

Preface

Last year I went to Saluce to fulfill my duty with the most famous and excellent Mr. Louis Gonzaga, the Duke of Nevers, who is my old teacher and friend. I was very happy that he had come to Italy, now the Lieutenant General of the Christian King Charles IX. A title that undoubtedly was due to him. He had earned it through his own valor and service rendered to the King for the space of twenty-two years. Namely, on a day when he was valiantly fighting, still only twenty-nine years old, and was taken prisoner at the battle of Saint-Quentin.[1] It might be enough to make him worthy of such a great office for the blood he had shed, only to return eight months later from his injuries to the battlefield in France among the enemies of the Catholic faith. He still suffers from these wounds which cast doubt on his life and his recovery to this day.

I will now return to my purpose. I found there the gentleman, my brother William, who seemed to be completely changed, and yet I had just seen him two years earlier in France. He was so weak and lean, withdrawn by the harsh handling of a very long quarantined illness and other sicknesses of his body. As he divulged deep sorrow to me, I could not for the life of me keep the tears out of my eyes seeing him in such a pitiful state hearing him draw out his words so softly and so weakly. For I love him not only as a younger brother but honor him as if he were the eldest. I did not want my pity for him to make him think worse of himself. I immediately resisted myself and with a more courageous countenance began to express hope that he would recover his health. His friends and our parents were earnestly looking forward to seeing him and I had hoped that he could receive the advice and counsel from a good physician from our city.

Shortly afterwards the Duke had come to see his cousin, the most excellent Princess Eleanor of Austria, and understanding William's desire to see our house again, he was content with his departure and let him come for a period of six days. We thought this would be a good opportunity to assemble the best physicians in the city. He was very tired and weary from the purgations[2] he had already undergone. With winter approaching, we thought it best to postpone the cure until spring, at which time he hoped to be in Italy during his Master's leave. He hoped to seek a remedy for his sickness and preserve himself from the discomfort and suffering, but also to spend the rest of his life in quietude.

While he was deciding what to do, in came our neighbor Master Anniball Magnocavalli and offered his assistance. Master Anniball is an excellent philosopher and physician for the diversity of Arts with which he is included and is counted in the number of those who are called Generals. His good behavior made him so acceptable that I was not surprised by anything he might say. After spending a short time with William, he woke in his heart by his delightful vision an extreme desire to enjoy more time of his pleasant company. Master Anniball was very displeased to find my brother in his current state of mind. Drawn by a sudden and mutual affection, they agreed to take the opportunity to visit each other as often as they conveniently could. So great was the courtesy of the Physician, instead of having my brother suffer the pains to visit him, he came to our house the next day only to find him at the table having just eaten. After that, they withdrew into a small room where I used to have a few books for show rather than for study. They passed a good portion of the day, which they continued for the next three days, with many notable discussions. My brother took the pleasure to recount each day's events to me in the evening. Their talks were so well seasoned, that I decided to preserve them for posterity. Ever since my brothers' departure, until the present, I have been gathering their discussions which resulted in what follows here.

Solitude

A conversation between
William Guazzo
and
Master Anniball Magnocavalli

William. I thank God, Master Anniball, for your visit regarding my prolonged and possibly incurable disease. To cleanse my miserable soul of this bad mood, he tends to my needs and comfort so that I can pass this illness with less discomfort. From this day on I do not doubt through the acceptable presence of Him, I will receive more help and satisfaction than I am capable of expressing.

Anniball. I have many reasons, Master Guazzo, to think well of you. Mainly I feel obligated to do so because I see that you deny your illness is from the hand of God, the good and powerful from whom all things come, and show Christian modesty by blaming yourself. That certainly is a thought suitable to the cross you wear on your chest. I will not praise you so, rather I must reprimand you a little and bear with me if I speak frankly because you call this your disease, an incurable one, you seem to distrust the one who sent it to you, and likewise cannot rid you of it. I will not blame or praise you for your opinion of my presence. You can assure yourself that instead of those signs of goodwill that I cannot show outwardly, I have an inner affection for you in my heart ready to do your service. I pray that you do not hide your condition so that I may understand it. I speak not as a physician even though that would be very useful to you in the future, but as a friend whom you should not hide your mishaps.

William. My brother has already promised me of you, all that can be asked of a skilled physician and a good friend. For this, I must return to Italy, in a more favorable season for the healing of the sick. I wanted to stay until then to open my wounds to you, and among others, those of the heart, which I feel oppressed by such a great melancholy[3] that in my mind I had good reasons to say that my evil is perhaps incurable, since all the doctors in Paris and France have not been able to help.

Anniball. For an ailment that disrupts normal bodily functions, it is necessary to stay until the winter is over to cure it unless your needs force you to use a faster remedy. For a disease of the mind, you must apply the appropriate remedies at all times, striving as much as possible to be happy and tread under foot all the irksome thoughts that bother you.

William. Certainly, as you advise me, I will gladly use all the time my committed service will spare me and all the free time that I may have, with a certain honest pleasure. With that in mind, I cannot forget or dismiss my troublesome thoughts.

Anniball. A person who is sick should consider the things that hurt him and those that help him, to the point of avoiding one and insisting on the other. It seems to me you remember things based on your experience; you have found that increase or decrease of this mental anguish or melancholy, as you define it.

William. I remember that I have clearly noted that the company of many is difficult to endure; on the contrary, solitude is a great comfort and makes my travels less difficult. And even if for the service of my Prince, I must socialize not only with other gentlemen (his servants), but also at Court, to converse and deal with many people from many countries and nations, yet I do so against the heart, and go ahead like the *Tortoise to enchantment.* [4]

Zeus asked the tortoise why she did not come to his wedding and her excuse was that she preferred her own home, so he made her carry her house about forever after. Engraving by Karel van Sichem, 1660.

7

I feel that it is a great journey for my mind, to understand the conversation of other people, to formulate appropriate responses to them, and to observe such circumstances, as the quality of the person and my own honor, which is nothing else but pain and overpowering. When I retire to my home, whether to read, write, or rest, I regain my freedom and let go of its reins, so that, being accountable only to myself, it is entirely applied to my pleasure and comfort.

Anniball. Do you think you will recover your health by continuing this solitary life for a long time?

William. I dare not say so.

Anniball. I now begin to fear less that this disease may be incurable.

William. And now I begin to know from your own words that you are that simple man as you told me you were. But if those who should have given me solace discourage me, how can I be a comfort to myself?

Anniball. Take heart kind sir because your illness is easy to cure.

William. You have in your hands the weapons of Achilles, with which you both wound and heal. Between these two contrary propositions, one is false.

Anniball. Both one and the other are true. Because all the physicians not only from France, but from all over Europe, not Aesculapius[5] himself, with any medicine, whether simple or compound, can without great difficulty give you the help you desire in this world, as long as you do not stop (as I see you do not) to proceed in your actions contrary to their prescription and mind.

On the other hand, I can also assure you that what you have told me, based on certain signs that I am beginning to discern in you, is that your disease is easy to cure. The medicine is in your own hands, so in a short time, it is possible you could regain your health. And to speak more clearly, I must tell you that to exempt yourself from this illness, you must first allow yourself to cut off the cause and origin of it.

William. How am I going to cut it off if I don't know the cause?

Anniball. I'll let you know, your illness is derived from the false image you have, like the butterfly that flies around the candle, you gladly accept your death. Instead of consuming and starving your illness, you give it nourishment. You think about receiving comfort through solitude: filling you with a bad mood, root in you; and there you wait ready to seek secret and lonely places, being conformable to their nature and disperse all your joy and company. Just as the flames hidden by a force holding them down are fierier, these corrupted moods, lurking in disguise, more forcefully consume and destroy the beautiful places in your mind. Therefore, I wish to dispel those thoughts of where you have gone and to repair that way of thinking so you can change your order of processing. Account loneliness as poison and companionship as the antidote and foundation of life. You should frame yourself in a manner to project loneliness as a concubine and to keep the company of others in your favor, as a legitimate spouse.

William. Yet I have heard many famous medical experts make this opinion that in order to have a healthy body, it is necessary to have the contentment of the mind.

Anniball. If that is true, then it is.

William. Goodness, if that's true, then it's no different from solitude which is good for the body because it recreates the mind. What do you think about that?

Anniball. I have already shown you that the pleasure of solitude considering your nature is counterfeit: now I will prove it to you. True pleasure, simply speaking, is what naturally gives everyone pleasure in general. And therefore, although solitude is pleasant for melancholy people, it is nevertheless unpleasant for others. You will understand better if you look at how some women with child have food cravings that others abhor. We would not say those cravings are convenient, because even though they please some women, they are generally unpleasant for all. And when the melancholy person and the pregnant woman are freed, one from their false imagination and the other from their altered taste, they will hate the things said above.

William. You make me doubt the worst case that I am aware of by indicating through your words that you include me in the number afflicted with melancholy, whose minds are so broken that they cannot distinguish between sweet and sour. I will not flatter myself, even though I have a whole mind within this crazy body, because my pleasure is very common as with other men of good taste. Some people like company, however, I know many of great value and deep knowledge who cannot handle crowds and prefer a solitary life, like fish do water. I am surprised by the definition you have given to pleasure, which is beyond the truth. Considering not just conversation, many other pleasures are acceptable to some and irritating to others. When it comes to games, dinners, concerts, and other delightful events many men shy away from them because they are more willing to deal with serious matters and are mostly men of good calling and not of the common type.

Anniball. God grant that I may never again doubt that your brain is disturbed, and if it entered into my thoughts to say it, and if I were to say it, then not you, but I would be considered ill-witted. Your reasons do nothing to conflict with my definition of pleasure, but rather confirm it. Those who do not like games, music, parties, and company, have by research and great contemplation or by some other accident, acquired a habit and a custom of being melancholy. In this world a greater number of them are found than the other. For this reason, in these pleasures mentioned above, they have lost their taste by chance, not by nature, while those pleasures are delighted naturally. For this very reason, we must establish this other foundation, that man being a sociable creature naturally loves conversation with other people. To do the contrary would offend nature itself, a fault for which many have done penance. For some, remaining locked in these voluntary prisons become ill-favored, thin, discouraged, and full of bad blood where their lives and ways become corrupted; almost to the point that some resemble the nature of savage beasts, while some lose courage and fear their own shadows. I will stop repeating to you what has happened to many people, who by living a long time in solitude, have fallen into such vehement and frantic fantasies, have on occasion been laughed at and pitied. In contemplating the things that writers write about concerning such men and the things that I myself have seen, I think there is nothing strange about a poor blessed soul believed to be transformed into a grain of millet, for a long time he did not dare to leave his room for fear that the poultry would devour him. It is not possible without great effort and cunning to remove the false image of this kind of melancholy person. There are others who have taken their own lives by means of water, fire, the sword, or throwing themselves headlong from above. Some at the end of their days by natural death have given testimony to their folly. As did the melancholy Athenian, who no less at his death than during his life, refusing the conversation of men, left these verses on his tomb.

> *Here I lie; I am no longer what I was before;*
> *Do not look for my name or you, who read,*
> *Go away with the pain that God gives you.*

It is good not to be alone

William. I am satisfied on this point and yield to your expertise that a solitary existence is not healthy. On the other hand, what pleasure can I seek from the conversation with others? When I meet another man of a similar mind, I give it one hundred percent, which either out of ignorance, pride, folly, ambition, altercation, or by unseemly behavior bothers and troubles me so much that both my mind and body receive great harm as well.

Anniball. I am not surprised at this, because the number of insufficient ones is much greater than that of the accomplished. However, it is your part, as much as you can, to leave them and support yourself in the following: to see our age and participate with the quality of iron. There is no one from the golden world that you can converse with. It is not amiss to call to mind that common proverb amongst our countrymen,

"We must not leave to sow corn out of fear that the birds will eat it up."

Likewise, we should not confine ourselves from going outside to do our business with men for fear of bad company. If you were headed from Padua to Venice, you would not miss the opportunity, because you would not embark on a vessel in which sometimes there are men, women, religious, clergy, soldiers, courtiers[6], Germans, French, Spaniards, Jews, and others of many nations and standings. That is why we must force our will, and sometimes satisfy it with what it does not like, which follows a virtue of necessity. On this subject, I will tell you that time and place have forced me to be present (rather with my body than my mind) in the company of those people, whom I could very easily forget because they are altogether different from my life and profession: from whom nevertheless, I could not withdraw lest I should be thought to take upon myself either too much gravity or too little courtesy. Although at first I was discouraged, later I went away pleased and joyful, seeing that I had framed myself in the moods of others. When I left the company I had kept, they thought very well of me. Likewise, when you become familiar with the course of the world and through prolonged use, you shall be brought to abide the company of such manner of people. You will perceive that if it is not good for your health, at least it will not hurt you.

William. I clearly perceive the understanding you have, even of things belonging to the virtue of the mind like the health of the body. I would be glad to hear such facts, if it were not disagreeable to you. I would be very glad that we were looking for a discussion that is most beneficial to the state of man, either solitude or conversation. Now, I would be reluctant at any time if you tried to convince me to take a medicine that might improve the health of my body and the sickness of my mind. I could never find in my heart to do this, on the contrary, I would sooner love to end my life in a desert with great disadvantage.

Anniball. There are certain kinds of spectacles that make things show greater than they are. Your courteous goodwill makes you go beyond the truth and to the best of my knowledge nothing compares to what you say. It is not so little to know that the gentlemen who warn and summon me to this fight are very well-equipped with weapons and courage. Nevertheless, without losing anymore time excusing my ignorance, I am ready to hear most willingly where your opinion is grounded, which seems to lean toward solitude. It is my intent to answer you, not knowingly, but according to the ability of my weak capacity.

William. Please do not think I'm signing myself up against you, as a subtle logician, I never learned where arguments came from. What I am saying is my own opinion, rather than from any judgment or learning.

My desire is to give you the opportunity to educate me a little. I am willing to understand instead of resisting because when you answer my requests, I derive great pleasure from it, so much so that I agree with the poet, Dante:

You content me so, when you resolve,
that doubting pleases me no less than knowing![7]

An engraving of Dante's Divine Comedy, Canto XI. G.
Zompini inv., and Magnini F., 1757.

Anniball. I attribute all this to your courtesy. In touching on this topic, let's do our due diligence to determine the effects of solitariness and conversation How many types are there and how they should be understood, we will soon agree and it will not be necessary to spend a lot of time thinking about it. First, I would like us to defer and suspend these several points and learn about this matter from a general perspective so that I may have the opportunity to enjoy your delightful and discreet perspective longer. But I will not forget (as someone who tends to your health) to remind you that it is not good for your sickly body to seriously occupy your mind to consider such matters so deeply. Many times the desire to contradict and to have the advantage in reasoning inflames, alters, and destroys the body and dilutes the matter; which would deceive many doctors, resulting in a different diagnosis from the ancillary information. Therefore, I advise you for your health and mine also, not to be too serious in this discussion so that I may be able to answer you more easily.

William. Sir, I am not one of those ambitious people who seriously want to be considered above others. I will simply tell you without affection those things that I have already heard from some virtuous people that will be dictated to me by a certain spirit of reason and then return to your sound and perfect judgment.

Anniball. I am very glad that our talks are quite familiar and pleasant, rather than forced and serious. Depending on the occasion, many times I protest on my part so that you can hear the proverbs, which the

Artisans have in their mouth, and those tales that are told by the fireside. I naturally live off such food and would like to give you the opportunity to do the same, and therefore also have an eye on both the health of the body and mind.

William. I promise to imitate you as much as I may as we enter into this discussion of differing opinions. First, to rise to the true service of God and enjoy those incomprehensible and eternal heavenly benefits that he has promised to his faithful; the deserts, all by places and solitude are the right path. On the contrary, groups of people are nothing more than hooks and words, which forcibly remove us from the course of our good thoughts, setting us on the path to destruction. That is why this life is full of suspicion, deception, lewdness, perjury, detraction, envy, oppression, violence, and innumerable mischief. A man cannot look away but will be forced to see evil or something other or similar that enters and infiltrates a wide path to the heart. Later they are planted as poisonous seeds, which grow until the destruction of the soul. This never happens to the loner, who is safe from all enticements, entanglements, and surprises; without love for the world is wholly raised up to the contemplation of their original and happy state. Likewise, whoever receives God's help by their prayers, must leave the company of others and retire to their room as God has expressly commanded. It is no wonder that God was pleased with the devout works performed by the first fathers, Abraham, Isaac, Jacob, Moses, Elijah, and Jeremiah. Neither should the example of our first father be less for us, who was happy while he lived in solitude since he felt miserable and sad when he was in the company of others. I have heard many people say that knowing that the vanities of the world and the conversation among men were impediments to the service of God and their own salvation. They have joyfully left their proud palaces, their great riches, their high degrees, the company of their relatives, friends, and parents, to shut themselves up in the poor Monasteries where they live the rest of their lives in holiness and patience. If the examples already cited are not valid for you, look at the works of Christ, who has made his prayers to God his Father, went up the mountain. His ascent was so fast, that he remained in solitude and entered the desert after the death of John the Baptist.

If we consider, besides the service of God, how much the solitary life is worth for our instruction and happy life, we can not help but curse whether it was Saturn, Mercury, Orpheus, Amphion,[8] or whoever it was that gathered and assembled in one body. The people scattered abroad in the forests and mountains where they followed nature instead of the law, not giving credence to the subtle persuasions of others, but their own guiltless conscience, and leading a loyal, simple, innocent life. They had not yet sharpened their tongues to slander their neighbors, given their mind to being cruel, nor had they infected and corrupted their manners with the contagion of vices which began to heat up in the cities and assemblies of men. That is why you see that naturally all people endowed with knowledge and virtue (to avoid the common kind which rejoices in the company of others) withdraw with great pleasure to secluded places, far from people, to have leisure for their appreciable and commendable contemplations. If this is true, as it undoubtedly is, that philosophers surpass all other men to the extent that light is better than darkness, it is a simple case to sail soundly into the deep sea of divine Philosophy. We must be careful to avoid the conversation of men, more than Scylla and Charybdis[9], who chose the lesser of two evils. They not only escaped the praise of the people but also shed light on the rejection of the rule of government and highlighted those great honors and offices to which ambitious men go all day with great effort craving and seeking. Although it may seem by chance that all men naturally desire conversation and the company of others, I remember the phrase you once told me that if you are an impartial judge, you should come to the same conclusion that a man should not reckon or account for the multitude of people who either by the desire of some vain pleasure, vile profit, or fickle and transitory promotions are always in the company of others and in conversation. The opinion of the philosopher should be followed, who on his return from the baths was asked if there were numerous men in them, to which he answered, "No." Shortly afterward, he was asked if there were a good number of people in them, to which he then answered, "Yes." Therefore, you must agree with me that if conversation produces pleasure or benefit, it is mostly for the ignorant and careless, for which loneliness is a kind of torment. Being alone, they serve no useful purpose but to count the minutes on a clock which they think is going too slow. Hence, the saying, *"Rest without learning is the death and burial of a living man; which never happens to the wise."* They only live when they are apart from others (not men, if I may lawfully say it) in which they get into this earthly paradise of solitude, where they feed their minds with the most pleasant nectar of knowledge. Neither is it ridiculous what Diogenes[10] happily and inexplicably did when he approached the door of a church while the people came out and pushed himself in the midst of them and eventually entered the church saying, "*It is the role of a man like me to always be against the multitude.*" This will demonstrate that we should, according to the poet's dictum, "*Follow the few and not the common crew.*" This is similar to the words from the philosopher Pythagoras[11] when he said, "*He did not follow the common way.*" I could say many other things in praise of the solitary life, which is by right and by reason singular. It alone is the good life acceptable to God and to pious men, the friend of virtue and the enemy of vice, the true institution and form of life. So for my part, I mostly remain alone, and always say in my heart (as the holy man said) "*The City is a prison to me and solitude is Paradise.*" I will stay here and listen to your opinions of the reasons that I have just mentioned.

Man was not born only for himself

*A**nniball.*** You have avoided nothing at all in this discourse from the duty of a perfect Courtier, whose job is to do everything with careful diligence and skillful art. Your ability to marry these skills allows you to hide the art of it. Everything seems to be done by chance, therefore being held in more admiration. By following that path you have elevated solitude, partly for reasons derived from your own good wit and partly from the doctrine you have learned from some famous writers, especially from Petrarch[12] and Vida[13], whose names and authority you have not mentioned. You hide those glorious doctrines which some educated men have discovered, always having their name on the tip of their tongue some philosopher, poet, or orator. Nevertheless, this ruse could not be covered up. I perceived it and therefore highly commend your discretion in judgment.

Now, since I have an opinion contrary to yours, it is up to me to answer point by point the reasons you have given. First, if I am not mistaken, it is based on the service of God and our salvation where in your opinion conversation is a hindrance, which I will firmly concede to you if you can show me that God's service is accomplished only through solitude. I am sure you will not deny that he has left us many commandments from his own mouth, the execution of which requires conversation. You cannot go to visit the sick, relieve the poor, correct and admonish your brother, or comfort the afflicted if you always remain silent. Therefore, if you want solitude to be used to appease the wrath of God and to obtain favor at his hands, you should say that it is beneficial and necessary only for the time allotted for prayer. Despite all that, I will not concede that it is a matter of necessity or that we should always be alone when we pray. When our Lord said that we should enter our chamber to say our prayers, it was said only to rebuke hypocrites who used to kneel openly praying at the end of streets with their solemn and false devotion to be contemplated, admired, and considered as men of a holy life.

We see that God has designated the church for Christians to assemble in, although devout and earnest prayers please him in all places. Nevertheless, we are bound to seek him out in the holy church ordained for that purpose. There we are moved to pray with more fervent zeal and affection, either by reason of the holy sacraments, which are often celebrated there or by the devoted prayers of others. Furthermore, we see that the religious do not separate their prayers, but by the ordinances of the church they come together in a single choir whereby uniting their voices, they make many minds as one, framing a harmony of divine praise and devout prayers, for the peace of God, for the salvation of humanity. That congregation not only calls men daily from their worldly works to divine service but also has great power and is very acceptable in the eyes of God. Whereupon some have said that it is impossible for the prayers made by many to not be answered. Neither does it detract from my firm opinion the example you propose; those who are fond of bodily pleasures become spiritual, the rich who have voluntarily entered misery, and from their majestic palaces, have committed themselves to miserable monasteries. Even though it appears they live in solitude, they are separated from us in this temporal life and still gather and assemble in their convents. They not only live and pray together with each other, but also converse with us by preaching, teaching, and doing other things that seem beneficial to our souls.

On the other hand, we secular men who have more enticements to do wrong must consider what God has given us, such as roses full of thorns, sweet with sour, and the understanding to discern their qualities and differences. Even though, as you say, that a person cannot see or hear the thing that makes the right way to salvation difficult and rough, a good Christian should not stray from it, keeping in mind the saying "*Every ease brings with it its discomfort*" or more simply put, *every rose has its thorn*. When he is assaulted by the temptation of pleasure or the annoyance of troubles, it is time to face the music, breaking those hooks and holds that you spoke of because you know we must enter into the kingdom of heaven through trials and tribulations. Although they do it wisely, whoever retreats to some obscure and solitary place in order to flee the fight of the flesh against the spirit, consider the great virtue and singular merit of a person, placed in the midst of pleasures, endures them and makes a conquest of their self. Think to yourself, how curious are these solitary people in their quiet world, who will neither see nor hear the complaints of others, share in our loss and our pain, are subject to insults, threats, blows, persecutions, outrages, dangers, and ruins, which this poor vale of misery is full of. Neither does the example of those first fathers work against me. They didn't live a solitary existence and they cared for their neighbors, which manifested with more deeds than you need to hear or I would like to say. I do not deny that Adam was happy while he lived alone, but for all that, you do not perceive that God in giving him company wanted to show us that he liked conversation. The last example of Christ contains in it a hidden meaning, different from the actions of men. In prayer, fasting, and mourning in the wilderness his meaning was, if I am not mistaken, to let a Christian know that from the fruits of those labors it is in their best interest to isolate their self from sin. By calling his wandering mind to this reckoning, it is to his advantage to keep it isolated from all other thoughts. If by the sadness of the face, the fasting of the body, and the prayers of the mouth, the heart does not pray, fast, and mourn, Christ is not imitated, but it is the act of a hypocrite, who, as the poet says, "*Covers their figures of speech with a cloak of deception.*" And if in addition to these works of Christ he had not spoken and it had not gone well with us, for that disputing, preaching, healing the sick, making the blind see, raising the dead, he spoke among us for many years with so many discomforts. In the end, he shed his innocent blood for our redemption. Seeing then while he lived among us, he left us an example and a path, which we should use in conversation. In my opinion, you were to blame for cursing him, that first with such discretion he gathered the scattered people, which had no knowledge of the vices that govern cities and towns. They did not combine the knowledge of science, honest and civilized behavior, friendship, craftsmanship, and trades that distinguished themselves from the beasts they used to resemble. Therefore, it can be rightly said that those who leave civil society to settle in some isolated desert, take the form of a beast, and in a way assume their brutal nature. So the common saying is that there is no other suitable name for a person living in solitude other than a beast or a tyrant. Because of this, he does violence to the beasts, seizing and taking possession of the forests, the tops of the mountains, their dens, caves, and hidden dwellings. Without seeing that the city and the assemblies of people are made to create the temple of justice, and to make laws that form to the life of man, which before was disorderly and imperfect. You then add that the educated and intelligent people do not account for anything but a solitary life, and you bring forth the philosophers who have contempt of crowds and are lovers of solitude. I could take a wide margin here to make you answer, but using all the brevity I can, I am just saying that these educated men of science love solitary places not by nature, but for their dislike of those they may be conversant. I grant you that there is nothing more disagreeable for the educated than the company of the ignorant. It derives from the great diversity and difference that there is between them. But as the learned flee from the ignorant, they willingly seek the company of other educated men with whom, moved by a certain virtuous ambition, they give proof of their knowledge, giving and taking the fruits of their labor they have gathered along their journeys.

You cannot name me any philosopher so tightly bound and rebellious against nature who, when time and place served, had no conversation either with his students to teach or with other philosophers to reason and listen to his reasons, who was not desirous to have other followers of his doctrine. Therefore, the work of Diogenes, which you have rehearsed, served well to show that a philosopher is contrary to the multitude, but not to disallow conversation, which he accounted of more than other philosophers did. This is why I conclude that while scholars and students love solitude due to a lack of respect for their fellow human beings, they will travel great distances to enjoy the company of those who are like them, whose books they have at home.

You allege in regard to those people who have rejected promotions and public office, thinking that it is something reprehensible to commit their free mind into bondage and be entangled with the cares of the world. There have been other excellent philosophers, who by their writings (which still exist) have rejected the opinion of the aforementioned. These alleged people without great reasons, devote themselves entirely to the study of science and contemplation; they completely abandoned those people who, by the law of nature, were obliged to help. They did not remember that man was not born only for himself, but for his friends, parents, and country. He seems to be too in love with himself or too far from loving others that he does not follow his proper nature to benefit others, even though they were born among them. Therefore, this sentence is well worth writing in letters of gold, *"He, who does nothing but acts of reproach, is stained with reproach."* Now, if all the praise of humanity consists in doing, according to the opinion of the philosophers, what is the use of this silent and idle philosophy of which, one can say as of faith, that without works it is dead, and is of no benefit to anybody? For the one who has obtained it cannot prove to have learned any science if he does not make it known and if other scientists do not recognize it. From this comes the proverb:

*Between buried treasure and hidden wisdom,
no difference is known.*[14]

An etching by Jan Luyken illustrating Matthew 13:44 in the Bowyer Bible, Bolton, England, 1791-1795.

And it can be said that these same men resemble the greedy that possess the treasure but do not have it. It is their fault that they do not practice what they know. In fact, just as music that cannot be heard is not taken into consideration, the philosopher does not merit the honor that does not manifest his knowledge. What Socrates knew very well, although in no other way deserved to be considered the wisest man in the world, deserved it only for this alone, that he was the first to bring moral philosophy down from heaven. Seeing all the philosophers bent to the contemplation of nature, he not only framed himself to obtain wisdom, live well, and teach others to live, but devoted himself entirely to bringing to perfection this part of philosophy, which is so profitable and necessary for our common life. He made the world see the open madness of those who prefer to hide a candle under a bushel, than put it on a candlestick. In addition, you know that those who do not like the company of others, however wise, remove them from their matters of learning, showing they are so insufficient and so foolish that they usually give everyone the opportunity to laugh at them.

I still remember the nonsense of a gentleman that I went to school with at Pad. He was not inferior to any of the other students at the university, but for the rest, you would have said that he had been one of those owls that are afraid of the other birds. His cluelessness led me to pity him, especially one day, having heard of the sudden death of his father, he went out and bought a pair of boots. One of the boots was so straight that it made his leg and foot very sore and the other boot was way too wide. We tried to tell him that he was being bamboozled, and he answered that he was aware of the faults in his boots, but the shoemaker had sworn to him that the one boot was made of such leather that would shrink from wearing it and the other from an animal hide that would stretch in less than two days. What do you think about that? Do you think a man like this could be called wise because of his education or a fool in respect to the common people? Therefore, it was rightly said by an ancient poet that *"experience is the father of wisdom and memory the mother,"* to show that it is necessary for him to obtain knowledge of things, not only what is provided in books, but also to have undoubted experience and practice in the understanding of human things. Having this knowledge must be received and remembered, in order to be able to advise him at a later time, to prove what he has already done, and guide him so that he may help others based on experiences encountered in the past. And if you know that this is true, consider that not only in the profession of us physicians, but in other careers as well, speculation without practice is by no means certain. We give more credit to an argument based on things, which we have tried out of reason, than in the mere doctrine of others. If you who have spent time experiencing life away from your own home, are able to judge how wise and discreet your journey has made you see how different you are from those who have never heard any bells ringing other than these. To show the bravery and wisdom of the great Ulysses[15], with good reason it was said to his immortal praise:

Many countries he had seen,
and in their manner was well seen.

I think I have sufficiently refuted your reasons, without

having to force myself or make an effort, as I could well do, to give you a more peremptory and weighty answer, which I will not. I think you are content with this since you have spoken of this matter, rather than to make me understand your great ingenuity, then to maintain in good earnest this opinion. The same people, who have taught you this false doctrine, have also taught you the truth, and I am sure that you are not ignorant that Petrarch, despite all the praises he attributes to the solitary life, did not have to learn that without conversation our life would be flawed, for he has been no enemy of good company. He frequented the Courts and supported many princes and gentlemen, I am not talking about Monsignor Vida, not because of the works he has written while in solitude, but because of the knowledge that he demonstrated in public. For a long time he used the Court of Rome and by his actions had shown others a good example of goodness. He obtained not only the authority under which he governed the flock entrusted to him for a long time, but also earned the title of a Bishop worthy of a higher degree. Moreover, he glorifies the solitary life with the intention of showing his great wit, degrading it later with various and invincible reasons. Among those he affirms that all the animals as soon as they are born will stand up and are capable of standing tall on their own, which nature did not grant to man who, as soon as he is born, needs the help and support of others. If this reason is not enough, nature has given man the ability to speak, not to talk to himself, that makes no sense, but to be able to communicate easily with others. You see that language helps us to teach, ask, confer, negotiate, advise, correct, dispute, judge and express the affection of our hearts: the means by which men come to love each other and unite together. He concludes, in the end, that a man cannot achieve any science unless taught by another.

Conversation with others is not only joyful but necessary for the perfection of man, who must confess that he is similar to the bee that cannot live alone. Therefore, following the opinion of the Stoics[16], it is assumed that all things on earth are made for the use of man. Man is created for the use of man. Following nature as your guide and helping each other to communicate common beliefs, it will be helpful to give, receive, unite and bind together, through the arts, their occupations and mental faculties; so that he may think himself unfortunate having no means of conversation to advance himself and others. That punishment is imposed by laws on some offenders as a kind of torment. For there is no greater affliction than to live among men and be deprived of their help and company.

Now to finish my talk, there is no pleasure here on earth that can be received without company, which made Archytas[17] of Tarentum say that if someone could by God's permission, ascend to heaven and once there behold the nature of the world and the beauty of the stars; that sight would not be as awesome to him if he did not have someone whom he could tell what he saw. You can then perceive that neither air, nor fire, nor water offer us more help in all our needs than conversation. But, if by chance all these things are not enough to prove this matter to you, I am willing to bring you (touching on this) many other reasons, as substantial as those already considered.

William. It is not surprising that lovers have no law or restraint in their hearts, as your Poet says:

> *The senses reign and reason is now dead;*
> *from one pleasing desire comes another.*[18]

Since I feel very comforted by your kind speech, nevertheless some doubts still remain. Like the mother-in-law out of extreme hatred does not discern the virtues of her son-in-law and the mother out of excessive love does not know the imperfections of her own son; you show yourself surprised with the same passions. By criticizing being alone and praising the company of others, you have not said the good that comes from solitary life, nor the evil that comes from the company of others. Therefore, to manifest and discover what they keep secret, my intention was not to defend and praise those people who moved either by some sudden plaything that takes their minds by some melancholy mood, rather than a good mood, withdraw completely into lonely places and pay no attention to what we do in the world. I consider them dead, or at least men who are not good for themselves or for others. Those who are not willing to put their virtues into practice for their own benefit or to teach them to others who need them. I usually compare them to the Fox, who prefers to bruise and break his tail against the ground without any benefit, then to give a little to the ape to cover his private parts. In the same way, I never wanted to deny that by frequenting the company of men, a man may do works acceptable to God. My opinion was, and is, that the perfection of man consists mainly in knowledge and solitude is more available than the company of others if I am not mistaken. As proof of this you see how those who concern themselves with the affairs of the world, for the most part, lack knowledge, and conversely those who wish to learn, do not seek it in public places among the masses, but in their studies and private rooms.

It is not a question of saying that some scholars make fools and imbeciles of themselves in public, because this foolishness is regarded to be only by the vulgar kind. They are seen as incapable of indulging new ideas: how to set their thoughts aside, how to dance in measure and follow the rhythm of the music, and how to compliment another person. According to the common people, he laughs at them with contempt and makes fun of them. But for all that, they are favored and honored among other educated men, who accept the simplicity of manners and the gentleness of their minds, what ordinary people call foolishness. Now let's turn the page, and place one of these scoffers in the midst of a company of learned men, and you will at once see him be speechless from his shame or speak to his dishonor. Let's say he is among certain educated people, who reasoned about the excellence of the poets, driven by his own ambitious ignorance, interrupted their talk by saying that, without further contention, "*Horace*[19] *was preferable to all the other poets. Petrarch had the same opinion and preferred him before Homer*[20] *and Virgil*[21]." Upon being asked to expand on the opinion of Petrarch, he responded with, "*Virgil and Homer had seen Horace alone against all the Tuscan.*" Then they laughed more heartily, more than your educated friends at the boot of a joke. Then the laughter started again when the fool was asked to show the meaning of Petrarch in those verses, when he added, that what he meant to say was that neither Virgil nor Homer nor all the Tuscany poets were able to encounter Horace alone. Now if this scholar was given the benefit of the doubt, he probably stumbled upon a corrupt persuasion in opinion. So I am led to think that learning without experience is more certain than experience without learning, and I would prefer to have the name of a simple scholar, than an ignorant courtier. From which I will infer that whoever obtains the knowledge and understands it must, as the craftsmen say, *"watch over the shop, and not walk in the streets all day gallivanting about amongst the people. "*

If you make the case that a lot of good things come from the conversation with others and weigh the good against the bad, the bad will outweigh the good by a great amount. Because the number of the good ones is so small and scarce, you will be forced to change your way of thinking, otherwise, *if you lie down with dogs, you will get up with fleas.* The Cretans[22] were very clear about this, when they wanted something bad to happen to someone, they would anticipate that he would trust the company of those who meant harm to him, so those bad things would come his way.

In addition to that, we have reached a point where you cannot behave yourself so well, but that you shall receive a thousand injuries, if not in life (which is not itself very safely warranted) yet at least in good name. And on this day, the malice of men is so great that they do not spare the honor of whomever it is, be it a Prince or a private person. They think menacing and preposterous thoughts about all the good works that are done so that if you devote yourself to the practice of charity, you are taken for a hypocrite. If you are personable and courteous, you are called a flatterer. If you help a desolate widow, you will soon hear a voice saying, "*I know what follows.*" And if through carelessness you determine not to be a friend, he won't talk to you anymore. If you are defending an oppressed person, be careful that you are not taken from your home at the wrong time. Do not think you will be spared if you belittle the profession of a soldier, because they will not limit themselves from just beating doctors and lawyers to hinder them from defending their clients. But to what end am I going to get lost in the intricate labyrinth of abuses and disorders of our time. I will go out immediately and persuade myself that vices should be banished from the world if conversation were removed. Are not adulteries, robberies, violence, blasphemies, murders and countless other evils learned from conversation and through it committed?

Learning never gets old

*A**nniball.*   You pretended to give in to me at first, yet you have risen against me with a second assault. But I will not stop trying other answers, to end (if possible) our controversy. You base learning on solitude and because of that, I must ask, from whom are the principles of science and learning to be obtained?

William.   From our teachers and professors.

Anniball.   You will then be caught in your own web, from these words that you grant me, the beginning and the end of learning depends on the conversation. Indeed, just as the armorer cannot be sure of the quality of a corselet[23] until he has seen it tested with a lance or harquebus[24], an educated person can not be assured of their knowledge until they have met other educated people and talked and reasoned with them so they can validate their capabilities. It seems clear to me, a conversation is the beginning and end of knowledge. But you add that men versed in the Court and commonwealth lack knowledge. I must remind you of this point, just as there are many sciences, arts, and professions so are the lives of diverse men, who as it pleases God, some enter the trades, others to war, medicine, or the law. This tends to support one goal, to achieve honor and profit by these means. These people divide their life into two parts: the first, to learn those things that can serve them till the end and the other is to put them into practice. For example, you are the Secretary to a Prince, and I am not unaware that because of the good parts that are in you, you must seek the reputation, independent existence, and consider the happiness of those who have been elevated to Cardinals and Vicars of Christ. Furthermore, to prepare yourself for that position you learned Latin and the Tuscany language, and many other arts necessary for this purpose. Your perfect writing style and great discretion in handling affairs have afforded you the reputation and name of an excellent Secretary. Others have a similar approach, among which there are some who devote their minds to agriculture or merchandise and are no longer concerned with learning but with reading, writing, and counting. And when they are among scholars, they are not capable of discussing meaningful rhetoric or poetry, nevertheless, they are not to blame, nor can we say that they are deprived of the knowledge of good writing because of conversation. From the beginning of their lives, they have decided not to meddle in studies. It's enough for them to be considered wise and well regarded in their own profession.

A scholar is worthy of being laughed at and criticized for dedicating himself completely to study. He does not frame his learning to everyday living and is completely ignorant of the affairs of the world. I will also tell you that it would be a great mistake to believe that knowledge is acquired more in solitude among books than in the company of scholars. A maxim in philosophy and experience shows that *learning is easier to obtain through the ears than through the eyes*. Someone should not have to dim their vision and wear out their fingers turning the pages of a book when they can see them present and receive by hearing the natural voice, which is inevitably imprinted on the mind by a wonderful force. On top of that, if you have the opportunity to read about a hard and dark place, you cannot ask the book to explain it to you, therefore you will walk away from it disappointed, saying if the book can not be be understood, I will not understand it. Of course, you know it is much better to speak with the living than the dead.

Once again I will note that the spirit of a solitary person becomes dull and weakened without anyone waking them up and asking some questions to touch on their knowledge and reasoning about it. By not comparing anyone with them, they attribute too much to themselves. On the contrary, the one who listens to others praise their studies admires them more, while those who are reprimanded correct their faults, and the one who is negligent is pushed forward by their counterparts who try to surpass them in glory. And since they think it is a great shame to stand behind their peers, they also consider it a great honor to be able to go before their superiors. But above all other things, the commendable controversies that arise among the educated have the most force to stir their spirits. By disputing what they learn and in that manner, they understand, explain, and remember it better. And while they argue for lively reasons, hoping to gain the upper hand, perfect knowledge of things is achieved, and so it is said that "*a debate of the facts is the filter towards the truth.*" Although the truth is taken from the common consensus and opinions of people, those opinions can only be known through conversation and the company of others. The poets wanted to show and infer that, even though Jupiter[25] was the omnipotent God, he called the other gods to advise them and listen to their opinions.

Put aside the fables, do we not know that the important and wonderful institutions of the Holy Church do not come only from the Pope, but from the holy general councils where they have been discreetly weighed and allowed? Furthermore, is it not the custom of all princes when it comes to the affairs of their estates, because they do not want to do anything on their own, bring their advisers together and determine matters according to their advice? Do not commonwealths, cities, and even small towns gather together to choose officers and establish laws by mutual agreement? Is it not customary for Magistrates to take the common advice and opinion of their assistants; and do doctors do the same in our assemblies and colleges where we make the decision regarding the healing of the sick by the advice and judgment of the majority? Did not Apelles[26] delight in placing his paintings abroad and secretly stood by to hear the opinion of the spectators, and when many were of one mind in criticizing a particular part, did he not fix it according to common voices and opinions? And didn't another painter say that the town was the teacher whom he had learned his art from? Finally, was it not useful for a wise Emperor (whose name I cannot recollect) to send spies abroad every day to listen to what was said about him, sometimes changing the manner of his dealings, and thus reforming his life from good to better according to the reports that have been made to him?

In truth, he who relies on his own judgment is risking too much. There is a common saying, *"He who does well, counsels himself well."* Therefore, the counsel is considered a holy thing. I cannot sufficiently express the great good which comes from conversation and from the knowledge which enters through the ears and sinks into the mind, coming from the mouths of scholars.

I would like to remind you of the honorable Academies and Universities that have been instituted for this purpose in many cities of Italy, among which we must not forget to speak of Mantua[27], founded in the house of the most famous Lord Cesar Genzaga[28], a mighty prince, and special patron of the learned; nor Pavia[29] which thrives prosperously by numerous students. But perhaps it is something worthy of admiration that in that small town of Casal the Academy of the Illustrati puts on such a gallant show. For the moment, now is not the time to mention their excellence, but to return to the matter in question. The fruit gathered by these Academies is inestimable, and they know what they are doing well, those that are educating their students and knowing that a person cannot obtain and learn too many sciences because the arts take a long time and life is short. Nevertheless, they can obtain whatever their hearts desire. Some discuss divinity, some humanities, some philosophy, some poetry, and other diverse subjects. They participate mutually and in common with what each one in private has learned after great pain and long hours of study. By the example of those who, not being able to live by themselves and make a good meal at their table meet together with their neighbors in one place. Each one brings their choice of food with them making an exquisite banquet. Therefore, it has been profoundly said that man is a god unto himself, for he receives such great pleasure and comfort from another.

This is represented by the image of the blind man, carrying the lame cripple on his back, who teaches him the way. The Alemanni[30] said:

Thus the whole of two halves were made,
The one lending his sight, the other his steps.

I say again, a conversation is the full perfection of learning and it is more useful for a student to have a discussion for an hour with someone like their self than to study alone all day in their room. By consulting with your companions, if you have misunderstood something, you usually come to the correct meaning of the matter, clear your mind of many errors, and begin to perceive that your judgment may be easily obscured by the veil of ignorance or some passion, and in a crowd, it rarely turns out that everyone is blinded. Finally, after the test, they know that the virtue and the knowledge found in books, is nothing more than a painted virtue, and true virtue and learning are acquired more with practice than with reading.

The time has come to respond to you, touching on the inconveniences that are incurred (as you say) by conversation, that make us deviate from the correct path, and alter our good intentions, by accompanying men of lewd behavior. Although in my imagination you may be satisfied with some reasons already alleged, I will say again that it is true, just as some diseases of the body are infectious, the vices of the mind pass from one to another, so that a drunkard attracts his companions to love wine. A man devoted to idleness and pleasure corrupts a brave man. The continuous conversation is so powerful that many times, against our will, we imitate the vices of others. It is said that Aristotle's friends and family had learned to stutter and Alexander's friends had acquired his rudeness in speaking. Do not doubt me, I have already said, pursuing the company of evil, a man by experience is a wolf of a man, not a god. According to proverbs, *"a companion of fools suffers harm"*,[31] and *"if you touch tar, it will stick to you"*.[32] But in the same case and for the same reason, virtue produces the same effect. And as a dead ember is lit, it ignites, so a bad person in the company of good people participates in the same manner as the good. Good air and a person's own land are beneficial to the health of the body, so are the conversation and company of good people for a sick mind. The sick leave some seed of their illness with those who cling to them and for the same reason the good leave behind their best to those who are around them. Just as a sweet smell comes from perfume to delight the nose, from the good a certain kindness goes towards those who need it, and most often it remains in them. That is why the foundation of your reasons is that in conversation a person cannot do good works, they will be heard and misinterpreted, adding insults, hurt, and damages to the subject matter, because they prefer the company of others. I grant you that the good order and manner of living in a certain way is completely lost, but the lack and perversity of others should never make you regret having done it well. Whoever speaks should never deal with the censures and reprimands that come from the blind community which is ignorant and takes everything with twists and turns. You ought to follow the allowable sentence of Epicurus[33] when he says, *"I never wanted to please because they do not value the things that I know and that is why I do not know the things they value and recommend."* You also need to consider by moving away from companionship and leading a solitary life so you will live in safety and be exempt from the insults of the wicked. On the contrary, pay no attention to it and assure yourself that for one ill-conceived word spoken in the company of others, you will receive a thousand living in solitude. Because someone will not mind saying, perhaps in all likelihood, that you have some filthy disease or that you have committed some offense that sheds light like a bat. Others will say that you are a heretic and that is why you escape from the company of Christians and they will seek to put you in the Inquisition. Others will call you an Alchemist or a money counterfeiter; and if all these suspicions fail, you will at least be thought of as timid, reserved, bizarre, depressed, or else a brutal beast. Most will flee the company of others when accusations like these are made. So by that means you will find yourself fallen, as the common proverb says, "*Out of the frying pan and into the fire.*"

In the end, you will return to an ordinary life, determined to move on and live well despite the wicked. Their naughtiness set against your virtue and goodness will make it more excellent and famous. You shall rejoice to see that your virtue has won the victory in the opposition, and persist in your goodness in the midst of their malice.

You must consider it deserves no great praise or merit to know how to be good among the good, however, there is worth being good among those who are bad. Also, you must think that among those false interpreters, there will be some upright judge and defender of your deeds. Though all men of the world should fail you, the high judgment of God will not. If in whom you shall place your trust, you may be sure he will hold his hand over you. He will defend you against the malicious and slanderous, and in spite of them will bring the truth to light and give it the upper hand.

I think I have fully answered you and therefore without any further discussion you may know that to get wisdom by the accomplishment of learning and to come to dignity, riches, and worldly promotions; conversation is expedient. To say that every man should have an eye only to his own affairs, is nothing else but to make man likened to animals. It is most certain that solitariness puts many evil things into our heads and makes us believe that which is not. It is nothing but a frightened enemy to nature and it is seen daily that a man being by himself is fearful and tempted to commit many evils; whereas being in company, is courageous. This, Crates[34] rightly signified when seeing a young man walk in a private place, asked him what he did there so alone. The young man answered that he talked with himself. To this Crates replied that the young man should take heed to not talk to some naughty fellow.

What more can I say, but that the herb Hellebore[35] may rightly be given to the solitary as to the fool. If they have no need for the company of others, they have no experience, if they have no experience, they have no judgment, and if they have no judgment, they are no better than a beast.

William. I think the northeast wind does not move the clouds in the sky as much as you have completely cleared my mind after chasing the mists that obscured it and made it wander and run for the love it had for solitude. I perceive the conclusion of your kind discourse seems to be that solitude should be taken out of the world completely, and companionship and conversation with others should be chosen for the health of the mind and body. Yet despite all this, I do not see how this can happen. There are times when solitude is needed and is necessary for the inner and outer well-being and prosperous state of life. I think it is appropriate and worth mentioning here.

Anniball. Do you not remember what I told you at the beginning of our talk, in order to clear the doubt and questions between us and completely resolve it; we must distinguish between solitude and conversation with others.

William. I agree with that.

Solitude can refresh the soul

A *nniball.* This is why I would tell you that from now on the time has come to leave our general discourse and come to the particularities that we have already proposed so that there is no confusion between us. I confess that solitude is not entirely guilty or banished and at some point, as you say, it is needed and necessary. Therefore, we must first understand that a person sometimes has company being alone and in solitude, and other times he is solitary among the company or conversation with others.

William. Pardon me if I interrupt, these discussions and distinctions seem puzzling to me. Therefore you must help me to understand them, instead of acting like Oedipus[36].

Anniball. I will explain them to you. First, there is a kind of solitude so rare and perfect that is always without the company of others and conversation, not at certain times. It pleases some devout men to enter, where they are altogether dead to the world, choosing the best part and living alone (if it can be said that those who are with God are alone) to end their days in the most pleasant way, in a most unpleasant life. This cannot be achieved by anyone without the special gift of God and whoever risks entering it exposes himself to a great danger that affects his own safety and has no respect for this phrase: *"Woe to the lonely man, who when he falls, will have no one to help him get up."*[37] I will make no larger speech of this lofty kind of solitude, referring to the long discourses the divines make of it, but descend to the less than perfect solitude, which is deprived of conversation only for a certain time.

I conclude that there are three types of solitude: that of time, of place, and of mind. The solitude of time is the stillness of the night or the moment in which one speaks to oneself in the presence of many. This type of solitude, as can be judged, is no less beneficial than necessary for all kinds of people, because of the things that are learned by word of mouth, both from readers and preachers, and is (as I said before) of greater strength and effectiveness than the books and writings of authors. Next, the solitude of place is the room or private house that everyone chooses for the purpose of isolating themselves from the company and conversation of others. Here we must consider that some settle in this solitude of place for various reasons. Some with the intention of raising their thoughts from worldly vanities to the contemplation of God and his marvelous works in order to rejoice in him with incredible joy and health of the soul, so they can understand in their mind what they cannot see with the eye. Some obtain the fruits of learning through study and speculation, and some to talk to themselves about public or private affairs. All these places of solitude, taken and used in due time have a great force to stir the mind and prepare them for an easier and surer address to the works and actions belonging to conversation. If we diligently consider the fable of Prometheus[38], Jupiter's ambassador on Mount Caucasus, with his heart torn by the Eagle, we will discover that solitude is depicted from the mountain and from the Eagles contemplation which wounds the heart and preys on it. Nothing else is signified by the conjunction of the Moon with Endymion[39], but that he spent many nights in the contemplation of heavenly things where he gathered the fruits of Astrology. And the shoulders of Atlas where he bore the weight of heaven, represents to us nothing else but the knowledge that he had of the superior world by means of contemplation.

These myths are the same, although they are solitary with respect to the place of where they are alone, they are in company regarding the diversity of things which they ponder in their minds. Thereupon, Scipio said "*He was never less alone than when alone*", having found himself in some place alone, he discoursed many things in his mind pertaining to the increase of his honor. Therefore, I must tell you that just as this type of solitude is useful and necessary for the disposition of the mind, so often it is harmful for the health of the body. This is why I told you at the beginning of our conversation that you should avoid it. Because the better the wit of a person, the more they beat themselves (from being alone) about pleasant and intricate points due to which their body can be led to various dangerous diseases.

I will not assert that this solitude of place is chosen by all to dedicate themselves to laudable studies and commendable speculations, because there are some who have their nose in a book full of lewd and lascivious examples all day long. They applaud and inure themselves to this doctrine and make it an ordinary practice. To the extent that these ill-disposed people may say that they have learned more antics by being alone than they would have done being in the company of public and frequented places. Praise God and the providence of our ancestors, who justly condemned such works as soon as they are published to fire as instruments for all lewd and naughty purposes. I must also tell you that there are some who choose solitude out of mental and bodily laziness with the intention of avoiding travel, affairs, and work that they should undertake for themselves and for other people. They loiter lazily submerged in delicacies in which they are preserved, not like musk in a box, but like swine in the mire. I have known some of these lazy merchants to withdraw from the company of others for most of the day, taking pleasure in doing nothing, unless it was to lie in their beds. Yet they will make someone believe that they have spent all of their time reading one good thing or another. I have never seen such fellows who act like this but let us consider the Emperor Domitian[40], who I suspect it may not work well for him because he takes pleasure in piercing flies with the point of his dagger most of the time. At least he does do a little exercise and prefers to kill flies rather than letting his mind be corrupted by idleness. If he was to be blamed for this, it is not for the little exercise that he does but for having left undone important matters befitting his greatness and useful to the preservation of his empire. We must conclude from this that, he who abandons the active life to embrace the contemplative life deserves praise, and he who being in the active life refuses companionship not from any honest occasion but from hatred of men, or from laziness, or from distrust of himself, or from some other fault and withdraws into solitude is most reprehensible.

Enough has already been said regarding the solitude of the place. It remains now to discuss the solitude of the mind, that is when one is present in person among many others and yet is absent in the mind and thought. Like a philosopher when talking with a babbling fool after a long and wearisome discourse, the philosopher said *"Sir, perhaps I trouble you with talking too much"*, *"No,"* said the fool, *"not even a little, for I was not listening to you."*

William. Indeed, I know many who have the skill with the eyes, the countenance, the gesture and other external signs, to make someone believe that they are very attentive to their speech, and yet have their minds turned another way, so that in an instant they are both present and absent, contenting both themselves and others.

Anniball. Although this discretion is common to many smart people, I remember that it is especially attributed to Madame Marguerite Stanga. This solitude had been figured out by a pleasant witted gentleman in her presence, who for the majesty of her looks, the excellence of her grace, beauty, virtue, demeanor, and her manners; seen by the other ladies of this city, if not with envy, at least with admiration. Although in her company he was present with a face, laughing and speaking, yet by the outward shining of her eyes revealing her inward affection, as if it were shining from the crystal that shows everything it contains. We see that her gallant mind, separated from mortal things, remains closed in on it, trying to exercise itself in more worthy and commendable musings. Taking from the world the opportunity to conceive any hope to win her to vanity, and on the occasion, the aforesaid gentleman wrote these verses about her:

While these happy eyes
gaze on the sweet beloved sight
of your beautiful, graceful, holy face;
Behold the sad soul
quickly sees, separated from her
are your high thoughts;
Wherefore I can well say, I will tell the truth
that I gave Margaret
death at one point to the other, and life to the eyes.

Returning to the solitude of the mind, I would like a wise man to enter it when he is in the company of the wicked. He should plug his ears from hearing their speech, as Ulysses did against the song of the Mermaids when he was walking among them, as they say, "*as those should among the thorns.*" We do not stop taking a journey because of a little rain or snow but prepare as well as we can to defend ourselves from bad weather. We must not delay the pilgrimage of ordinary life for the hindrance of the mischievous, but arm ourselves with an invincible mind against the evil dispositions of others to whom we must not give up anything at all. I told you that I would also mention Diogenes, who had some ingenious answers that he made on this subject. Among others, he was accused of having used the company of obscene and naughty people, he said "*The sun shines and spreads its rays on unclean places and yet never defiles itself.*" Another reproached him for something similar, and he replied, "*The physicians spend all day with the sick and yet are not infected and in truth, ill conditions take no hold of an honest mind, and a virtuous man does not care to be in the company of the wicked who have no power over him.*" As the proverb says, "*Surely in vain, the net is spread in the sight of any bird.*"[41] While being among them he realized that he is not there and according to the gentleman, to whom Aesop tells while in his study, there came a fellow who asked how he could live so alone. His answer was, "*I began to be alone even since you came here.*" Meaning to show that a learned man is alone when he is among the ignorant, from which he is divided in mind. It is now time to stop talking about this matter now that you understand what kind of solitude is helpful and necessary and how sometimes it is used in the company of others.

The nature and quality of conversation

***W**illiam.* I am satisfied with that point and would gladly have you bring this imperfect speech to a perfect ending. It is not enough to let me know that conversation is profitable if you do not go any further and show me what kind of conversation is necessary to obtain the commodities you have rehearsed.

Anniball. What you say is very true, but when we have spoken of the nature and the quality of conversation our discussion is linked together, it will not be finished because it is necessary to ask the general points that all people must observe in conversation. Once this is done the work will still not be finished since we do not apply a single medicine to all the ailments of the eyes, we do not use the same type of conversation with everyone. Therefore, we must handle the particular types that pertain to all kinds of people. Therefore, if you want me to distinguish piecemeal parts of the plant: stem, branches, leaves, flours, and fruits from the roots of this tree, I leave it to your consideration if this can be done in one day.

William. Since this is a profitable and pleasant matter, I beseech you that in these three days that I have to stay here with you, we may use the little free time you have left from practicing on your patients. You can show me all those things that belong to a conversation so when I encounter someone of any vocation and condition I can be sure not to omit anything that I ought to perform.

Anniball. I cannot fully satisfy your wish, for many reasons. First, to search for all the particular points of a conversation, as a matter, if not impossible, would require a lot of money to accomplish. We must consider that, as the philosophers say, there can be no certain and determined science from particular to particular. The particulars of conversation are known to most people of average understanding. I would do you wrong and think of myself speaking superfluously, even when I should be talking to those ignorant and unskillful people if I should ask earnestly of things so ordinary and common. Therefore, it will suffice to address the things that are mainly required in conversation, with which we will perhaps have the opportunity to mingle and join so many other things, which I have no doubt will satisfy you.

William. Truly, I see at this point that the diversity of matters that occur in a conversation and because of the difference in the life and manners of the people whom we converse with, you will take on journeys and costs much greater than the twelve labors of Hercules.

Allegory of the Twelve Labors of Hercules Statues in a Circular Garden, Matthaeus Greuter (German, Straaburg ca. 1566-1638 Rome), mid 16th-17th century.

Considering that people differ from each other by the degree of age, nature, life, manners, and profession, it is difficult and tedious work to fully and absolutely establish each one's own duties and whoever will frequent their company. I believe that once we have prescribed some form of conversation for all, we will not be done with it, because we must respect not only the difference between one class and another, but also between people of only one kind. Young people differ in behavior from the old, and gentlemen from yeomen[42]. Young people also differ from each other just as an old person differs in behavior from another old person and a gentleman from another gentleman.

61

Anniball. Since these differences are manifested in all kinds, I will briefly set out some general and more necessary means. Whereby, all can be reduced to one law concerning the form required for a conversation with people of different status and conditions which we have already mentioned. So as not to deceive you, understand that my meaning is not to discuss formally of their duty, nor to present to you all these moral virtues which belong to perfection and the happy state of life.

William. Why defer talking about such a profitable issue?

Anniball. Two special cases hold me back. First, I know that not only the Greeks and the Latins, but also all other nations have filled the world with many volumes full of precepts of philosophy.

William. The more books on philosophy we have today the fewer philosophers we have. Please tell me the other case.

Anniball. The other is that if I were to give a full and perfect discourse of moral philosophy it would not hold up except to those who have a deep understanding like you, with the intention of speaking in particular conversational manners for all sorts of people. It behooves me to have an eye on the common benefit considering that most people are not only devoid of intellectual and moral virtues but also lack the wit or will to receive them. It would be vain and improper, if not foolish, to go and teach the aforementioned virtues to such kinds of people.

William. I agree with what you have said and in case it is time for you to visit your patients, this would be a good time to take a break. If you like, tomorrow we can take up the matter here or at your house, the choice is yours.

Anniball. If you don't mind, I can stay here with you a little longer. We cannot choose a more suitable place for our purpose than here. The beautiful view of the various paintings recreates our minds marvelously and ministers the occasion of witty discussion.

William. Go ahead for as long it pleases you. I assure you, I have never heard a more delightful and harmonious discussion than this one.

Anniball. Therefore, since your question was what kind of conversation is necessary to achieve the perfection of which we have spoken, I will separate all other types and propose, for this purpose the civil conversation.

William. What do you mean by the word civil?

Anniball. If you want to know what I mean, I must first ask, do you know any citizen who lives uncivilly?

William. Yes, mother Mary I do, more than one.

Anniball. Now let me ask on the contrary, do you know anyone that lives civilly?

William. Yes, very many.

Anniball. So you see we give a broad sense and signification to this word civil. We understand living civilly is not said with respect to the city but to the qualities of the mind. As I understand it, civil conversation has no relation to the city, but to the consideration of the manners and conditions that make it civil. Just as laws and civil ordinances are distributed

63

not only to cities, but also to villages, castles, and the people subject to them. Civil conversation pertains not only to people who live in cities but to all kinds of people from any place or whatever calling they are.

In short, my meaning is that civil conversation is an honest commendable and virtuous way of living in the world.

William. I know from the exposition of the word civil that the field in which we have to enter is very wide and spacious. Therefore, I am ready to listen to things full of variety and novelty, then familiar and pleasant.

Anniball. Like Mariners, they first get to know the signs and tokens of winds and storms, sights and locations of rocks and shelves. In this way, they are able to foresee anything contrary that would hinder navigation and anticipate impending danger. They know how to avoid danger and choose the right times and places to navigate them properly. Thus, being eager to fully understand what civil conversation is with the intention of following it, we must seek to know what uncivil and blameworthy conversation is with the intention of avoiding it. Truly, we should avoid bad company, as well as, the harm and bad conditions that can be caused by it and for the judgment and opinion of others. That is why we are viewed by the company we keep. There is a common proverb that says, *"Tell me who you go with, and I will know what you are doing."* It was not long since the academic Frances Pugiella, a skilled lawyer and pleasant companion, told me of an undoubted sentence written by a famous lawyer. *"Much credit ought to be given to the deposition of a witness who gives proof of the*

honesty or dishonesty of a person, having seen him in the
company of others of a good or bad reputation. "

Now, I do not want to be blamed if in seeking out the
bad company I make a certain distinction of people
according to my own view and not to the common and
ordinary distinction of others. I consider the nature of
man in one way with respect to himself, and another to
the conversation he has with others. Considering only
conversation, I conclude that there are three types of
people that can be called good, bad, and indifferent
until we meet with words more proper and significant.

William.   Why do you think those terms are not
appropriate enough?

Anniball.   For two of these terms, good and indifferent
do not express the sort of men which I mean. To show
you more clearly, I will give you an instance of healthy
men. Those who have the *four humors*[43] equally
tempered in them, in addition to the other parts we call
compound and instrumental, which are the outer parts
of the body, are so well proportioned that nothing
exceeds its just measure. This type of health is rarely
possessed but by a few people. In spite of that, we
commonly call some healthy, who do not have such a
perfect constitution and are able to live and work most
of the time without physical stature and are more
sound than sick. Likewise, when I name the good I do
not mean someone so perfectly good that they have no
faults, in a manner as rare on earth as the Phoenix. I do
include in that number all those which are well
reported and reputed of in the world who come as
close as possible to the excellence aforementioned. In
the same case, when I said indifferent I did not mean

that they are half good and half bad. As a certain historian believes, talking about the emperor Galba[44], calling his disposition indifferent while comparing his virtues and his vices together because it was difficult to judge whether he should be counted among the good or the bad. I was referring to those who, although sprinkled with some imperfections lean more towards the good than the bad.

William. I can see now that these names do not quite express your meaning.

Anniball. We may find more appropriate terms in our discussion. In the meantime I say that we must always follow the good, avoid the bad, and never follow or avoid the indifferent. If I were not afraid of breaking your Boccaccio's head I would call the good desirable, the bad intolerable, and the indifferent tolerable.

Avoid the Intolerable

William.   You will offend Boccaccio with the improper use of the unusual words. For my part, I like the latter ones better than the first. As the proverb says, *"Second thoughts are always the best."* Please continue if you will.

Anniball.   The intolerable and the bad with their apparent faults are singled out and considered infamous, whose company we must absolutely avoid. The whole world would not be enough to prevent the rest of the world to judge those that frequent their company to be like them.

William.   The abuse of the world is such that many horrible vices have become familiar and common to the point that it is a fault not to have them and not to know how to practice them. This is why I am of the opinion that if we are going to give up company with the wicked we will only have a few left to deal with, insomuch that we would be inclined to change conversation into solitude and descend to the particularities. You know how serious offenses are committed against God, by means of blasphemers, which today are driven to such abuse that there are few or none who confirm not what they say with this wicked and detestable swearing. They do not think to beautify and detail their speech, as an orator does with illustrations. Neither am I in a position to tell you how a young gentleman, a friend of mine, was mocked at court for his greatest annoyance. He was always swearing by taking God's name in vain. In the end, to be accepted as a good courtier he was urged to stop this disdainful speech and deliver himself to the good work of the saints.   What I say about swearing I also reference many other heinous faults which are found in most people today. That is why they are common, I am afraid it does not make sense that you have prescribed to avoid bad company, and if I may say so, *"We are all stained with a pitch."* Those in appearance look like innocent lambs are indeed ravenous wolves and are worse than those who are counted as the most evil. Even the infidels and those who do not believe in Christ will counterfeit holiness.

Anniball.   We have become weaker in virtue and stronger in vice than our predecessors. I see that you have read the verse from the poet Horace which says: [45]

Quintus Horatius Flaccus

Worse than our grandparents' generation,
Our parents' then produce us,
even worse,
and soon to bear still more sinful children.

I am not surprised where in the past there were few who would blaspheme the name of God; in this day there are many who will not hesitate to tear him limb from limb, and be thought to be a drunkard or simple-minded who cannot swear vigorously. If you ask me why these people are tolerated despite the fact that they are much worse and more worthy of punishment than others of an evil life. I will tell you what will happen and why we do not recognize them. Offenses committed against God are something that does not affect us but pertain to God alone to revenge. We cannot remain silent when either our friends or we are hurt by someone's words or deeds, so that therein we esteem the creature above the creator. You will notice that such a person who speaks God's name in vain publicly would not dare open his mouth to reprimand the Prince or magistrates.

William.   I believe that they offend and commit no fewer disturbances than those who crucified Christ.

Anniball.   I think that they offend more because they thought they were doing well. Otherwise, they would have refrained from doing it because they know they are doing wrong. They do not stop and you know how much more heinous those faults are when they are committed out of malice than those done from blind ignorance.

William.   Hurry, I beg you to show me if we should avoid the conversation of these same people and if you put them among the intolerable.

Anniball.   These horrible swearers who make a profession of it when their blood is not stirred or for their pleasure rather than being moved with anger or any other occasion should in my opinion be classified in the role of the intolerable. For others, as a Christian, you should avoid them. As a courtier, you cannot separate yourself from them, not because of the large number of them or for the error of the world which considers them in the ranks of the tolerable. In short, we must consider that our name depends on general opinions which have such force that reason is of no force against them. Therefore, we must avoid those who have a mark on their forehead and are openly known to be dishonest.

William.   What would you say if I frequented the company of such, posed as a physician to cure their illness and as someone jealous of their behavior?

Anniball. If you think that you are able to help them in a better way, you will perform an acceptable act to God and to the world while in their company. The one who wishes to reap the good of a conversation must seek everything that can be had from those who may be improved by him or else can make him better. These people I talk about have sacrificed their souls to the devil and have abandoned all concern for their honor and opinions from them. They are so far away that you would become a convert rather than a converter. You must imitate the good archers who do not shoot all the birds, only those that are within reach.

William. Which people are you referring to that have a mark on their forehead and are intolerable?

Anniball. Those who for notable reasons are hated by the world, some for suspicion of hearsay, theft, usury,[46] and other misdeeds which must include ruffians, prostitutes, flatterers, gamblers, cheaters, and such.

Due to the baseness of their condition and their profession are considered infamous such as sergeants, executioners, and torturers. In addition, those who differ from us in religion such as the Jews and the Turks, etc. To be brief, all those who have a bad reputation and oftentimes for their misdeeds have been newly baptized and have such repulsive names that most people avoid their company like an infectious disease. I think it is a great shame to be seen among them.

William.   How should I behave with someone I know who is much meaner than those you have mentioned? They are considered to be honest people in spite of their deceptive hypocrisy.

Anniball.   There is a common saying, *"He who is bad and taken to be good can do a lot of mischief and no one believes that he is the one who did it."* Nevertheless, I put these people with the tolerable, because even if your conscience troubles you to come in their company, you give them the benefit of the doubt. They are not considered bad and at this point, we should satisfy others before ourselves and give place to common custom.

William.   No doubt custom is a great tyrant and I don't know why it should prevail over reason. The river Po, king of rivers, which is closer to us since there has been no resistance against it for the last six years has advanced and gained so much ground on this city that at length it has broken the walls and now threatens to overflow over them. The violence of custom, much like the river, is so overwhelming that it has conquered reason everywhere on this side of the mountains. I noticed on my return from France recently that the people are falling into a freer more decadent lifestyle than ever before. Throughout the towns, you will find gentlemen spending their time in the marketplace, playing cards and rolling dice with as much freedom, as they used to do in their private homes.

Anniball. You are not telling me anything strange. You should not be amazed to see these same playing games openly in the streets than to see the French, as I have heard, drinking and partying in the streets and taverns. I am convinced that if a gentleman, more precise than another, withdraws from these games and is condescending amongst them will be mocked and called disdainfully a wise man, doctor, poet, or such like that. I would like you to know that this new manner of life in the countries of the Piedmont has some color and meaning. You know the ones you have visited for many years, where soldiers from many nations have gathered, the people have not only become warriors but also retained the customs and rites of war.

William. Are you then of the opinion that a gentleman should converse with such people?

Anniball. On this point, there are two contrary reasons for me. If I respect the common use of the country which has now become ancient and has very deep roots, we must include them among the desirable and boldly use their company. On the other hand, if I were to consider this gaming life offensive and a bad example, and gentlemen in all other countries who behave well would consider it a shame to be in these public places with cards in their hands, perhaps some would place them among the intolerable. However, between these two extreme reasons, I see one in the middle of them, which makes me think that these people must be counted as tolerable. Even though they have been using this gaming abuse, you will find they do not apply it to this purpose which other players who make a profit from it; but for the pastime and recreation of it and besides we know that the rest of their lives are as modest and virtuous as any other people. That is why I think this custom of playing should not be judged by the world as good or bad. These people should not be rejected for seeking out honest company with others.

William. In my opinion, this is a kind of an injustice by allowing them what is inhibited for others and giving them the power to make a vice, a virtue. I understand your meaning that just as it is lawful only for the Cinganes[47] to rob, they also have the privilege of playing in the open street. I think the streets and public places should serve the common people for merchandise and the gentlemen for jousting, tournaments, shows, and similar activities which belong more to good horsemanship and military discipline than cards and dice do. That is why I am persuaded that they have nothing more to say in defense of their customs. Diogenes said it best when asked why he ate openly in the street, because he was hungry. So, they play there because being there creates the desire to play.

Anniball. There is no help in this but you must settle yourself to like such people with their imperfections. Every nation, land, and country by the nature of the place, the climate of the sky, and the influence of the star has certain virtues and vices which are proper, natural, and perpetual to it. Since good and sharp wits flourish where the air is pure and subtle, dull and gross heads are found where the air is foggy and thick. Touching on certain conditions, you know that the Greeks are singular in learning and eloquence, yet are also disloyal and untrue giving meaning to the proverbial saying, *the Greekish faith*. Moreover, there are other people who by natural virtue are given to the industry and discipline of war and by natural vice are driven to haughtiness and drunkenness. While some can easily sustain and endure pain, observation, and torment, those on the other side are vain and boastful. For some, sturdiness and devout holiness have always been proper and natural which are nonetheless worldly and inconsistent.

I am sure you do not doubt that we Italians also have some natural vices and virtues, and we do not exceed less in one or excel in the other. It does not seem surprising to you to see these various fashions and customs according to the diversity and the great distance of countries. Consider how much we differ within the borders of Italy, in the Roman, Tuscan, Lombardy, and others regions of it. Hold one of those regions apart and cast your imagination to the center or point of Montserrat and see how the Po and Tanaro rivers make countries differ in language, clothing, life, and manners which are no more distant from one side or bank of the river than the other. You will need to grant me that all countries have their natural faults as well as their virtues. You can be assured that if other people have not developed the habit of playing cards and dice openly, they will have brought publicly and privately much more pernicious vices. Now, so as not to waste any more time on this point, I will tell you that it is not inconvenient but necessary to follow the dissimilarity of manners and customs according to the variety of the countries. Imitate Alcibiades[48] who was praised because he had such a ready wit that he adapted himself to the diversity of the life and manners of other countries. As Saint Ambrose[49] put it, "*When in Rome, live as the Romans do.*"

Straddling a very fine line

William. Now would be a good time to discuss the general points related to a conversation with the tolerable.

Anniball. It is better in my mind to talk about some other things that have just come to my mind touching on the intolerable. Even though this matter is so broad that someone cannot speak enough about it, we must not quietly ignore the vice of slander. Those with the falseness of their tongues seek to tarnish the reputation of others.

William. This fault is so common throughout the world today, which is why it is difficult to avoid it even while we grit our teeth. Gossip spreads and swarms from the tongues of people in greater numbers than bees do in July which is why people cannot escape their sting, nor try to avoid it. People today take so much pleasure in this vice that many are free from almost all other faults yet are not able to restrain their blasphemous tongues.

Anniball. I have learned from long experience; commonly the idle, the ignorant, the unfortunate, and the bankrupt, who are not successful in their own affairs, are the ones who seek to deprave the works of others by speaking badly of them for they, themselves, do not know how to do anything well. This fault is common to many, and they are grateful and yet hateful to the world for its use. If you take a thorough look at it, you will notice that the fault of the one, who speaks ill of his neighbor for the intent of leading him to hatred, is greater than the one who takes bread out of the mouth of the poor. The soul is more valuable than the body, so it is a greater offense to take away from someone the good name that comforts the soul than to deprive someone of the food that sustains the body.

William. It seems to me that some contradiction is implied in these words, where you say that speaking ill of others is both grateful and hateful to the world.

Anniball. No, because our nature really makes us want to understand the imperfections of others, and we consider it the greatest pleasure there can be. We like to hear people speak ill of others but cannot tolerate it when spoken of ourselves, whether it be right or wrong.

William. I do not consider it strange that we do not like to be criticized ourselves. What do you think is the reason why we are so happy to hear people speak badly about others?

Anniball. I think this happens by the means of two

powerful enemies which we keep in our own house, namely envy and ambition. They conspire against ourselves, forcing us to grieve that others are considered good and make us desire that only we seem good. Let me tell you one thing that will indeed make you marvel and think against all reason.

William. What is that?

Anniball. There are two principal kinds of these foul-mouthed people, the one bad which you must lie about and the other much worse whose company you should not avoid. What I mean by bad is those who have no fear, no shame, without any respect or difference. They sharpen their tongues to tear apart and impair in all their talk both public and private, undermining the good name of others sparing no one, either present or absent. These same people while recounting the faults of others offend the minds of the listeners far more than those who commit them. Though they have a mark on their foreheads and are known as an infamous person for how much they utter their venom openly and plainly, they should be pitied rather than blamed. They clearly show that their horrible speech is derived from their own corrupt nature, not from those who speak badly about it. For this reason, their words are not believed and in my opinion, they do nothing but raise dust to get rid of them in their own eyes. In accusing others they condemn themselves and would have men regard them as popes only to show their selves to be fools and beasts. What shall we say about those cur[50] dogs who, without barking, bite us in private but should still be admitted into the conversation? Notwithstanding, they are considered far worse than the other.

William. What do you consider them to be?

Anniball. There are many kinds, but they all shoot at the same target. I call some of them maskers, rhetoricians, poets, hypocrites, scorpions, traitors, forgers, biters[51], mockers, and some unknown.

William. You make me laugh with your pleasant and strange distinctions but who do you call maskers?

Anniball. There are certain glorious fellows who at confession go with a mask on their face, yet they would gladly be known for what they are. Likewise, certain people with foul mouths hide under the mask of modesty. They will not name who they reprehend, yet evidently, expose him so all listeners know who they mean. The example of the countryman, who, in telling the hunter that the scout had not gone that way, nevertheless pointed out the place where it was hidden. Some of these maskers also use speeches with a certain outward show of commendation, nevertheless full of reproach and mockery. Those, according to the proverb, *have honey in their mouth, and a knife in their hand.*

William. Who are the rhetoricians?

Anniball. They are those who with a certain notability, called by the Masters of Eloquence, Dissemblers. They pretend that they do not mean any harm, yet do so, and even worse. Touching on this point, just the other day I was in the company of people like this and one of them, complaining of another who had verbally hurt him, said, "*I will not repeat the obscene part he played with a poor maid (whom he named), nor the beatings he did to another one night, nor the usurping contracts he made with some*

80

poor people which I am well aware of. I will say nothing about any of this, so I am not thought to be as bad as him." After them, come the blasphemous poets, who using the figure of antiphrasis[52] and speaking in contradictions will give in mockery the name of beauty to a woman who is filthy, and of honest to one who is a harlot, and will praise the eyes of one who is cross-eyed.

Let us now turn to the foul-mouthed hypocrites who under the cover of grief and compassion, in order to be better believed, lamentably rehearse misfortunes of others. This vice is very common to many people, however, is more familiar to certain women, who meeting with other gossips after the initial greeting immediately break into these speeches, *"Have you heard of the sad affair of my unfortunate neighbor?"* She then tells the story of how the husband through a trusted servant, caught his wife in her hasty business. Then they tell how the lover escaped down the wall and how the husband cruelly beat her and her maid. They leave nothing unsaid and add to the story with their own exaggeration. After that, another begins to say, *"And I will finish your story with the same circumstances that happened on our street this past week, but I beg you not to repeat it any further."* Now I leave you to think how in telling these good stories, they pass from one street to another to tell the doings of others, what purpose do they serve?

William. Last year the Duchess was forced to part with one of her principal women for this very reason. She continually had her hours devoutly in her hands and had long been regarded as a woman of a very pious life so that she had risen in great favor with her highness.

However, over time it was discovered that she had a malicious and slanderous tongue where she set about bringing all the ladies of the court into disgrace with the duchess. Before getting to the heart of the matter, she used an insinuation like this: *"Madam, I would not want your Grace to be offended or disturbed by what is happening to your gentlewomen, for you must think that we are born sinners and that there is nothing in this world more fragile than our flesh. "* Consider for yourself how much she inflamed the Duchess with these words, with a desire to understand the rest. As she urged her to continue her tale, the naughty queen humbly requested her not to oblige her to speak of such inconveniences. After enduring three or four assaults at length, as if forced, rubbing her eyes from the grief which were full of tears, she began to relate the devious pranks of the gentlewomen and never finished her reports of reproach.

Now I'm waiting for your speech from the ill-tongued scorpions.

Anniball. Those are the ones who will say these or similar speeches about you or anyone else, "I do not think it is possible to find a more courteous and honorable gentleman than Master Guazzo, whom I would hold in such high esteem if he didn't have but one great fault." You know how afterward when speaking badly about you it will feel like a scorpion has just stung you with his tail. Others will handle the matter more artificially saying, mischief takes those ill tongues that will not stop molesting those that are good and honest. They will not even spare the good name of our Master Guazzo. Although he is the flower of courtesy and virtue, they continue to say that he is proud and malicious and because he is corrupted by money; has done and said such and such things, and more.

William. I understand. These same people can go hand in hand with those who always accompany their "*yes*" with a "*but*". What do you say about the ill-tongued traitors now?

Anniball. If by chance you received some harsh treatment at the hands of your prince and to relieve your stomach you complain about it to someone in confidence who in turn tells the prince. Would you not judge him to be an ill-tongued traitor who deserves your disdain?

William. Yes, indeed. This fault occurs in courts frequently. Often, princes desiring to know the truth have allowed their servants to fight against each other. I know that on such occasions some gentlemen have taken themselves to some neighboring place where one would not live with the name of an evil speaker and the other of a false accuser, they have put an end to their lives and their quarrels together.

Anniball. Under this withered branch, I also understand all the tale-bearers, spies, coiners[53], sowers of discord, and those who betray the secrets of others. What type of punishment would you give to these offenders?

William. The least punishment they deserve is to have their tongues pulled out, as Jupiter did with a certain nymph who betrayed her secret love to Juno[54]. I am not surprised that many people fall into this category because we naturally chase after the things that are forbidden. A certain wise man once said, *"It was easier to hold a burning coal than a secret word in one's mouth."*

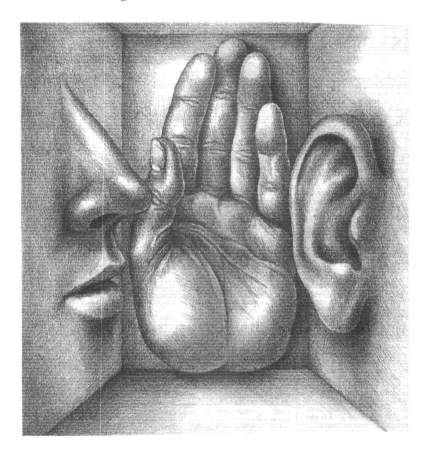

That is why I consider him to be a fool who reveals his secrets to another if necessity does not compel him. According to the saying, *he subjects himself to another when he tells his secret to one who did not know it.* I remember, for this purpose, a pleasant story of a servant whose master gave him clothes. No sooner after he received them, he gave them to a friend of his. His master confronted him for it, and the servant replied, *"Why do you want me to keep them when you cannot keep them yourself?"* A man can give us the same answer by revealing our secrets, which we ourselves could not keep hidden in our hearts. We must take it for granted that the things that are entrusted to the ears are for the most part proclaimed in the streets. Just as it is a great fault to reveal the secrets of others, on the contrary, it is a notable virtue to know how to keep silent and keep one's tongue in check. If we are bound to keep the secrets of a friend, how much more must we, as secretaries, conceal the secrets of our master who gives us a salary to be secret? We imitate the Greek, who when told that his mouth stank, replied that the cause of it was the many secrets which he allowed to mold and mildew in it. This can be understood not only of other people's secrets but also of our own. Indeed, whoever wishes to keep his thoughts secret and not reveal them to anyone becomes their own secretary. I think I have strayed from our path, and therefore it would be better for us to return to the distinction of the ill-tongued.

Anniball. On the contrary, your brief and sententious[55] discourse served its purpose, and I listened to it willingly as a matter not proceeding from a secretary imploded in trivialities. Let us discuss the ill-tongued forgers, whose malice is such that they will accuse you of having done or said what you never thought. That is why you are often harmed by two people. From the false accuser, who, according to the proverb speaks words of reproach to someone who is deaf. That is, slanders the one who is not there and the one who, before understanding the case, gives credence to these false assumptions. This lack of questioning is too great a fault and in a number of these forgers if you talk to them about something soberly and wisely will make a false and perverse interpretation of it and give it a bad meaning. Then there are the ill-tongue biters, whose mouths are accompanied by short nips that pierce our hearts more than sharp arrows. Even though they quip and scoff a lot of times according to the truth, they are not free from guilt because they do it with a spiteful mind where they incur blame and ill-will. They are so indiscreet and insolent that they would rather give up a faithful friend than a mocking speech. Nor can they conceal their words under the guise of pleasantness or seriousness so that their maliciousness is deciphered. They are worthy of blame because such taunts provoke men to anger. When provoked, they return one scoff with another, and those answers are always worth two of those made without provocation. We have a thousand examples of this, among others, the one known to most people would be the one made by the emperor Augustus. He met a stranger by chance who resembled him very much. He asked him if his mother had been in Rome at any time insinuating that he might be his father's bastard son. The stranger answered him no less boldly than merrily, *"My mother has never been there, but my father has."*

William. It is very true that he, who says what pleases him, listens to what displeases him.

Anniball. After them come the mockers and scorners, who, without any grace, make a mockery of everyone and easily persuade themselves that they are pleasant and merry conceited fellows, than they perceive themselves to be ignorant and inconsiderate fools.

William.   A gentleman will not easily accept being mocked by one of these glorious asses, nor will he easily digest such an insult.

Anniball.   I think so, but he must have patience and follow the philosopher, who, when he was told that some mocked him, replied, "*It may be that they mock me, but I am not mocked.*" No doubt he is greatly deceived who thinks that he is allowed to despise or mock anyone except those that are evil. Now there remain those who are unknown with bad tongues who work their deed in two ways, either by writing or by illustration. The first, liable for slander to undermine the honor of others. These same people cast their rancor against princes and great lords like lightning striking, burning the tops of the towers and high palaces. The other, with tablets and pictures used to represent men and women in some infamous and dishonest act.

William.   I remember that in a famous city the most natural and resembling picture of the gentleman with two horns on his forehead was placed on his door at night.

Anniball.   Such actions are atrocious and deserve punishment rather than blame. You have heard how many kinds of ill-tongues there are in the world and how grievous are their faults. It is more shameful when it is committed against the dead. The person manifestly shows his vile and abject mind, offending those who cannot defend themselves. They did not dare open their lips while they were alive. From this, a saying arose, "*Even a hare, the weakest of animals, may insult a dead lion.*"[56] It is time to bring this discussion to an end. I fear you will judge me to have an ill-tongue for speaking so badly about those who have an ill-tongue. All these kinds of evil speakers gathered together, though they are hated, are not commonly excluded from the company of others. They are not branded on the forehead, so we cannot refuse their company, but we must try our best to avoid them.

William. Since you have no intention of running away from the conversation of these annoying people, I think it would be appropriate and necessary to learn a few tricks to keep us from the venom of their serpentine tongues.

Anniball. Your request is very reasonable. Just as certain animals when dealing with snakes will eat certain herbs that have the power to suppress and deaden their venom. We frequently have to deal with these culprits and should be armed with some preservative. For my part, I have no more presentable remedy than, when one of these foul-mouthed railers addresses someone, we should lower our eyes and not take pleasure in his insulting speech. If he sees that we are not taking pleasure in his words, he will refrain from that type of speech. You know that arrows do not stick to stones, nor do their rotten roots stick to them, but if they find the ground soft and suitable they will continue. Furthermore, if we diligently seek what is the greater fault, lending an ear to an evil speaker, or speaking ill of another we shall confess in the end, as others have done, that we are not able to give a determinate judgment about it. To tell the truth, whoever lends an ear to a slanderous detractor gives him an opportunity to offend and there is a good chance that he himself is of the same character. Thus, the one who speaks and believes he does no harm, or at least, if he does, he divides it down the middle, giving one half to the listener and taking the other for himself. So, like two blind men who lead each other astray, they both fall into the same ditch. Let us stop listening to the words of these people and in so doing we shall restrain their unbridled tongues and gain great honor and credit with the wise.

Just as it is good to not take part in the bad report of others, it is also a deed deserving commendation to not acknowledge the slander that others make about us. We must be prepared to have our ears as readily at our command as they have their tongues. By the example of Alexander the Great, while making war against another king heard one of his soldiers speak ill of him. He rebuked him sharply saying, *"I give you a salary to fight my enemy, not to rail against him."* The same Alexander, understanding that someone misreported him, did not seek revenge, but wisely replied with princely modesty, that it was proper for a King to do well and to hear ill. Moreover, the saying of Augustus, who hearing that Tiberius was very sorry that he behaved so modestly and patiently towards those who spoke ill of him, wrote these words to him: *"Do not, my Tiberius, follow your youthful fancy and take it in such scorn that there are some who will speak ill of us, for it is sufficient if we are, in that case, that no one can do us harm."* He also said to another concerning this matter that in a free city, men should have free speech.

William.   Not all princes have the courage of Alexander or Augustus.

Anniball.   Truly, if it is wrong to undermine the renunciation of individuals, it is far worse to disparage princes, especially our natural and legitimate Lords, and those who do so should be hated by all men. Speaking ill of them provokes them to anger and often gives them occasion to alter their conditions from being gentle and courteous, and they become rough and cruel. Nor can they excuse themselves by saying that there are mischievous princes and tyrants, inasmuch as they have received the command of God to obey their rulers, whoever they may be. In confirmation of this, it is said, *"If Nero is your prince, do not rebel against him."*

William.   Now that we are done with those prickly thorny tongues, do you have any other kind of people who should at least be endured and tolerated in our conversation, even if they are not desirable?

Flattery, the good, the bad, and the ugly

***A**nniball.* A certain philosopher was asked which beast he considered the worst. He replied, "Of the wild ones would be the ill-tongued; of the tame ones it is the flatterer." I think we should proceed in our discourse very orderly. Having already spoken of those wild beasts, we should now deal with these tame ones whose breath is so venomous that it poisons the hearts of those that listen to them.

William. Which type should I put them in?

Anniball. There are two kinds: one open, the other secret. The open flatterers are those compelled by need and hunger rather than by anything else. You bring them into the houses of great people, and they play their part so well that they make them believe, such as the sayings that *"Glowworms are lanterns"* and *"The moon is made of green cheese."* At least they will be sure

91

to say or do something acceptable to them. They receive the name, not only of flatterers but also parasites and buffoons. When Alexander complained of being bitten by flies and was eagerly brushing them off, a man by the name of Nicesias[57], one of his flatterers who happened to be present, said *"Beyond all doubt, those flies will be far superior to all other flies, now that they have tasted your blood."* Another, seeing Dionysius[58], beyond the reach of his hearing, laughing with some of his acquaintances, began to laugh too and when Dionysius asked him why he laughed, he answered, *"Because I know that all your words are so full of wit and pleasantness that they will make anyone laugh."* You also see in the theater of both the past and present, flatterers and parasites who by reason of being pointed out as they walk along the streets are noticed as an infamous person. They should be avoided as intolerable men of vile condition and of no valor, and who often like slaves are well and truly beaten for their scurrilous and broad jesting. And as the ape, who is not fit to watch the house like a mastiff, nor bear the burden like an ass or horse, nor till the ground like an ox, devotes himself to make us laugh with his pouting and sulking, and endure a thousand villainies. These flatterers have no honest or profitable trade to promote themselves worthwhile, so they go out of their way to delight the eyes and ears of others to their great shame and reproach. Then come the secret flatterers, who, under the guise of friendship and goodwill, cunningly and artificially insinuate themselves into the favor of others, and by their cunning wiles and false persuasions, cause them to make many mistakes.

William.   I think we should include them in the

numbers of the tolerable.

Anniball. Just.

William. I would rather argue that they should be put in the number of the desirable.

Anniball. Why so?

William. Though all reprove flattery in word, everyone commends it in their heart. I promise you that among the many cities, countries, and nations that I have traveled through, I have yet to find a man so fierce and savage who did not suffer to be cajoled and clawed with the tickling of flattery. Through my experience, I have noticed that all people of great worth and of the best minds take a singular pleasure not only in flattering others but also in being flattered themselves. You are not ignorant if you, wishing to extol me, came and told me that I was a strong wrestler or an excellent musician, I would think you were mocking me because I have no skills in those matters. If you are commending me for being a fair writer with a pure style or for anything else concerning my profession, out of politeness and modesty I will have the courtesy to accept your praise, but in my mind, I shall be well satisfied. I am sure that whatever you say about me in this respect is very true, and I am naturally desirous of being praised and commended. I remember reading that Themistocles[59], when asked what words spoken on the stage pleased him most he answered, *"Those that tell of my praises."* This desire is common to all men who are lustful of honor that to merely hear them exalted makes them exceedingly happy. Like Demosthenes[60], who, passing in front of two water carriers and hearing them say softly to each other:

93

"Here is the famous orator Demosthenes", turned around and stood on tiptoe to make him better seen, like the one who says, *"I am he."* What shall I say about Demosthenes? How many people are there who, without measuring their merit, without examining whether they are rightly or wrongly praised, willingly allow themselves to be deceived and take the praise for granted? On the contrary, how many do we see, and perhaps I myself am one of them, take it badly and somewhat angrily if they are not magnified. I will tell you again that if one of these parasites you have mentioned would begin to praise me and be inclined to present me in the best light he could, I would become emboldened. I would willingly listen to him, making me believe that although he flatters others, he has been clear with me. Yes, I would thank him for that and I wish all my friends and relatives were present to hear him.

Goodness, flattery is the way to make friends and gain preference. I am convinced that if you do not know how to gloss over things and flatter, you do not know how to behave in the company of others. I once heard a French gentleman say to his friends, *"Flatter me and you will give me the greatest pleasure in the world."* And there is no one who does not know that, just as bitter reprehension is the beginning of enmity, gentle adulation is the entrance into friendship. I am of the opposite opinion if you think that flattery tends to make people do wrong. Someone who is worthy of praise is more likely to be encouraged to do good. When someone sees himself praised without earning it, they often recognize their unworthiness and endeavor by their deeds to become worthy of such praise. If flattery were a fault, discreet parents and schoolmasters would not use it with children. They do not speak, read, write, sing, dance or any such like exactly and perfectly, yet their parents or teachers do not cease to praise what they do in order to encourage them to do better. You also see that nature has implanted a certain form of flattery in the hearts of little children, who run to embrace their parents and friends when they want to get something from their hands. Nature has also taught it to beggars who, in order to have our charity, pester and flatter us with beautiful words and pitiful discourses.

Moreover, consider these fine orators with their pleasant speeches, teaching men to insinuate by means of colorful words that sneak into the heart, to win the favor of princes and magistrates. Nor will I omit the example of tactful lovers who, in order to win their affection, address them in words both spoken and written: sometimes their mistress, love of their life, their soul mate, their hope, and other flattering names. Yes, they will not hesitate to send her to paradise giving her the title of a goddess and calling her beauty angelic and divine, her teeth pearls, her lips coral, her hands ivory, and as the Poet says,

> *Her hair is glistening gold,*
> *Her face as the driven snow,*
> *Her lashes so lovely,*
> *Her eyes two stars do show.*

To make a long story short, the world, is full of flattery and is sustained by it and is more in fashion than groomed beards or great ruffs[61]. You see how people in

95

order to avoid contention and be acceptable in the company of others calm one another, not only by words, but also by holding their peace, seeming to acquiesce to the words of another. We often use double diligence in some of our actions. If we see the clothes of our master or friend are very clean without a spot or stain, yet to gain thanks, we will not refrain from rubbing and wiping them with part of our coat as if there were dust or dirt on them. There are still some who, while others are talking, yet without caring in the least, nod their heads, lower their eyes, and with signs seem to hold up their yeas and nays, which is nothing else but flattery. You also know that we naturally hate critics and philosophers who at every word oppose us. They engage in futile tasks and say things such as *"seek knots in bulrushes"*.[62] However, on the other side, there are those who consent to our sayings, either in words or gestures. We consider them our friends, bear them great affection and love to be in their company, taking their flattery instead of courtesy and goodwill. Inasmuch as we hold it to be envious or proud, it does not reassure us in all things. Our vanity is so great that when people praise us, though we think it is far above what we deserve, we attribute it to the great abundance of goodwill than the fraud of flattery. You will never hear anyone lie to another for praise after being slandered unjustly and falsely, but, being puffed up with pride and vainglory with a joyful look he answers, *"The goodwill you profess to me makes you say that."* Therefore, not without reason, a certain flatterer, advised, to tell the truth, replied, *"A man must tell the truth to those who want to hear it; but who is this man?"* Bear in mind that, just as truth attracts hatred, flattery wins love and breeds respect.

If you take flattery out of the world, you remove all humanity and courtesy. We should not salute our enemy, even though he bids us a good morning with his mouth, because he wishes us much sorrow in his heart. What do you want a man to do? We must, by his example, give them merry looks, and laugh in their faces. We must play the fox with foxes, and delude art, with art. Just as it is a fault to fight with a friend, it is a virtue to know how to give way and yield to him. For these reasons, I must conclude that to win favor and happily achieve our purposes, we must always say complimentary and pleasing words, and must consider it commendable to extol both by words and signs the actions of others, and to give them what each one longs for.

Anniball. You have very ingeniously praised and expounded flattery, but I have a different opinion than you do. I will not be thought of as a flatterer and will oppose the reasons you have alleged. First of all, for the most part, people are flatterers of themselves, making themselves believe they are what they are not. Princes are often blinded by this folly, as was Domitian[63], who was neither afraid nor ashamed to call himself Lord and God. Of whom a flatterer writes these words to his glory, but to his own shame, *"The edict of our Lord and God."* Likewise, Alexander also suffered this madness in his head. It was not enough to be a man and a king and have the title of Great. He wished, in the name of God, to be called the son of Jupiter and was not pleased with those who did not appease him in this. A certain philosopher at this divinity, who had no skill in flattery, mocked his physician while preparing a broth for his supper when he was sick said, *"Our God has put the hope of my health in a bowl of broth."* Those who love themselves, without measure, willingly listen to flatterers because they think they are being praised when in truth are just being flattered. Therefore, there is no wonder that flattery is so accepted. Notwithstanding, discreet people, who know themselves and their merits, although they naturally desire to be praised do not like to be flattered or praised without reason. They think false praise is nothing but mockery, so I do not think you are so eager for glory. If in recital of your praise I mix in something that is not true, you would not thank me for it, you would either openly blame me in words or in your heart secretly.

William. See how you are wounded with your own weapon, for in commending as someone who does not like to be praised above what I deserve, you attribute a virtue that is not in me and shows yourself to be a flatterer and a flouter[64].

Anniball. You deceive yourself, and it is you who have received the injury. Having said that if a flatterer praised you, you would not take them to be a flatterer of you. Not allowing me to attribute to you a virtue which you think you have, you are contrary to yourself and make me appear to be a true friend and not a flatterer. Besides, when I say that I regard you as a person who does not seek praise without merit, this is not a compliment but a good opinion I have of you. This would be a compliment if I absolutely asserted that you are one of those who pay no attention to flatterers. Therefore, since my words have no meaning of praise, they cannot receive any interpretation or suspicion of flattery.

Continuing with our purpose, I say again that the wise man never accepts the false praise of flatterers, who resemble in everything coral polyps, as they change color according to the object they find, they change opinion according to the appetite of the listener. They are termed by an ancient author, *"enemy-like friends"*. Under their pleasant sugary words, they conceal a bitter and poisonous meaning such as the hook is hidden under the bait or the serpent among the flowers. They are no different from the butcher who scratches the pig with his hand, while having the intention of conveniently bringing his hammer down on their head. Can flattery be said to do any good? Does a person who is praised without cause endeavor to deserve it? The cunning flatterer puts the clothes so artificially on the back of them, whom he disguises with everything, that the seams are not seen. He commits himself to things that appear to be true so that they may be taken as fact. Some famous writers have sought the means of discerning a friend from a flatterer. In my opinion, it is very difficult, not impossible, to arrive at that knowledge both because the world is full of these tame beasts, and it is difficult to discern the evil that resembles good. Therefore, it was well said by a wise man, *"As the wolf is like the dog, so the flatterer is like the friend."* We must be careful not to make a mistake, lest we think to put ourselves in the care of the dogs and fall into the devouring of wolves. If you sense the smell of false praise, you will not feel in you that remorse and desire to desert (leave) what you speak of. This false praise has the appearance of truth and is bestowed upon you as due and deserved. I now come to the example of parents who, as you say, flatter their children, to encourage them to virtue. Children, on the other hand, flatter their parents to get something out of them. These two cases differ. The first is not in truth flattery because there is no deception in it.

William. Do you not deceive a child when he has only made a small leap, and you tell him that he has made an excellent leap?

Anniball. It is a good kind of deceit that tends to do good and is profitable to the party deceived. We physicians sometimes deceive our patients by giving them pomegranate juice instead of wine.

William. Let us examine the example of children who flatter their parents to get money or anything else.

Anniball. If I am not mistaken, this requires further examination. We must first understand that some, in order to gain favor, are in the habit of supporting and extolling what others say without contradicting anything. Others, on the contrary, continually fall into contention and contradict the words of others. Between these two extremes there lies a way for those who wish to neither soothe nor oppose altogether. We should in an honest manner know how to allow or disallow the words of others at that time and place, as it is proper for an honest person to do. Next, we should note that those who hold up everyone's yeas and nays, only with the intention of delighting should be called jesters, but when they do it for their own advantage they are definitely flatterers. According to this distinction, children who embrace their parents to obtain something from them must be called flatterers. In this case, we must further consider that children cannot give praise or show love to their parents which may exceed their natural and bound duty or which may be more than their parents think they have deserved.

William. Yes, but it is a common saying, *"He who flatters you more than he wanted to, has either already chosen you or is about to."* Parents are not so blind that they do not see in this case the subtlety and cunning of their children.

Anniball. They not only perceive it, but also conceive well of it and do not consider it crafty as you do not consider it as a job as you do, but rather a commendable thing. The parents see their children following nature as their mistress, which teaches us to humble ourselves in our need, and to implore others by deeds resounding with their praise. They also exhibit our affection for them and know that he who wants to have must ask, and he who wants to enter the house must first knock at the gate. We should at all times praise our heavenly Father. We are more inclined to do so both with the tongue and the heart when we desire to obtain something from his hands. To appease his wrath, we do not call him just, but make mention of his clemency and mercy, which we are in need of. From this we can rightly conclude that such actions should not be called flattery, and that infants, as well as children of sound mind, cannot, even if they want to, use flattery towards their parents. This was clearly demonstrated by Pittacus[65], one of the seven wise men of Greece, who said, *"Never fear to be considered a flatterer* *of your father."* And concerning the example of the poor who beg for charity with flattering words, I answer that necessity has no law. In order to avoid hunger, robbery is suffered in some countries, all the more reason that flattery is born in all. Besides, I do not think it is proper to call it flattery. A flatterer is not in the habit of showing his needs openly, but cunningly endeavors to induce others to be generous to him. For the same reason I support the cause of the orator, who openly asks the prince or judge what he wishes to obtain. He is not to be blamed more than someone who says, *"Take heed, for I wish to strike you."* Just as the latter shows his intention and gives his adversary time to prepare to defend himself, so does the Orator when he enters the scene without the judge first knowing the request he is going to make and thinking about the means that will be used to make his point.

Now all that remains is the last example of lovers, who I am happy to confess are actually no better than flatterers. A far greater man than I confesses as much, writing that if his beloved is flat-nosed they call her kind; if she is hairy they call her princely; if she is dark they consider her manly; if she is white, heavenly. This is not surprising, since lovers are both lawless and naive in their hearts, as our poet says:

The senses prevail and reason is subdued.

As the lover flatters his mistress, she flatters herself, for there is no woman so deformed who, hearing herself told that she is beautiful, does not believe it or at least does not think she is esteemed such by her lover. Take the example of the crow and the fox, so that the crow would give credit and consent to the praises that the fox gave him, he dropped the prey from his mouth.

The Fox and The Crow, Wood Engraving, Thomas Bewick (c. 11 August 1753 – 8 November 1828).

So many unfortunate women have felt the evil that comes from flattery. The breath of praise, like a feather in the wind, has allowed them to rise so high that not being able to support them there; they have fallen to the ground. In the fall they have lost so much of their honor that from lovers, they become servants.

Now, as to the point of civility and courtesy, where you say we salute those who are our enemies, I say this sentence is very true. We must not take all those for doves who say *"Peace be unto you"*, but we must call them dissemblers rather than flatterers.

William. In my mind, you give many names to one and the same thing, because flattery is never without pretense.

Anniball. There is a lot of difference between these two, as there is between the general and the special. It is true that he who flatters pretends, but not vice versa. Let me explain it to you. Look at a fencer, who, attacking the head of his enemy, strikes him in the leg or some other body part. You might say that this fellow dissembles, but not that he is a flatterer. Do not brave captains deceive the enemy when they boast of going one way and then take another route? Are victories not achieved by strategy and policies of war as well as by force of arms? What kind of counterfeiting is not objectionable, but rather commendable? Not only between enemies but also friends and acquaintances can one tolerate dealing colorfully with things that are not prejudicial to them. For instance, if I am asked to go to see a comedy or a play, or the like, and I do not intend to go there, I will pretend that I am sick, or if I do not want to be seen at night, I will disguise myself in some way. You see then that dissembling stretches too many things, and to many ends, and flattery is stricter and contained under dissimulation, as the special under the general. Wherefore I conclude that as it is not lawful to dissemble in flattering, because it does not harm the person to whom it is used, so it is permitted and cannot be said to be wrong to conceal without harming and without intent to hurt another. I readily admit that if they pretend to love someone, with the intention of deceiving or harming them, there is much to blame. The philosopher considers him worse than a counterfeiter because there can be no friendship where there is counterfeiting. But if, for reasons of civility and good manners I greet someone I know well without showing the slightest affection for him, I must not be called a dissembler because it is out of courtesy than goodwill that I honor him.

Besides, you know that the world is full of bad men who we justly hate for their imperfections. It is not good to let them understand the ill-will we bear them. Keep in mind that many are loved but not honored, like children who are loved but not honored by their parents. On the contrary, many are honored who are not loved. Then you have some princes, who are not loved by their subjects, or some magistrates, who are honored but not loved by the people. Therefore, we often cannot and ought not to fail in civility and courtesy, in regard to our own duty. We are bound to salute those who salute us, whether they are our inferiors or our equals. If they are princes or magistrates, or our superiors we ought to honor them out of the reverence due to their position, if not out of affection.

I think I have sufficiently shown the difference between feigning and flattering. Now I say again, returning to flatterers, they are people of the vilest and meanest nature. Although it is difficult, as we have already said, to discern a friend from a flatterer, we should note that commonly the greater are flattered by the lesser. The more prosperity they have, the more they are beset by flatterers, who are always directed to where there is profit to be reaped. Hence, it follows that princes are always besieged by these evil spirits. Whereupon Carneades[66] said that the sons of princes never learn to do anything well, but ride a horse. Their governors and teachers seek to please them and make them believe they are sufficiently educated in things where they have no skill. Of course, this is not the case in riding horses, for the horse, which is not a flatterer and has no more regard for the great than of the small, throws them to the ground if they are not able to sit firmly on the saddle. Therefore, we must beware of such people, both because they are hurtful to us, and because God is displeased with them. I do not know whether the offense is greater for the person who slanderously rebukes the good or flatters the evil. I have long since learned that God is grievously offended to hear anyone who is like him to be disparaged or one unlike him to be commended. No doubt, it is a great fault, by way of flattery, to commend for one thing that he should rightly be rebuked, which is indicated to us by the phrase, *"Woe be unto you which call the evil good."* These flatterers are like those who put a pillow under our heads, and soft and delicate feathers under our bodies to make us sleep.

Likewise, those who flatter in order to hurt are at great fault, as Judas did. Therefore, it is written that it is better to be beaten by a friend than kissed by an enemy, that is, by a flatterer. In conclusion, to commend what is bad in someone is the action of a deceiver and a kind of treason. Therefore, it is worthy of praise that Emperor Sigismund[67] who hearing a certain shameless fellow call him God, raised his fist and boxed him on the ear, and when the fellow asked, *"Why do you strike me, Emperor?"* He answered, *"Why do you bite me, flatterer?"*

William. As much as you have shown me clearly how hateful and hurtful these flatterers are, I think it is good to classify them among the intolerable.

Anniball. On the contrary, let us set them even

Anniball. On the contrary, let us set them even cheek to cheek by the evil tongued, upon the seat of the tolerable. Considering them both as friends, let us beware of them as enemies. Let us put a helmet on our heads to defend our ears from their perilous speeches, remembering that he, who willingly listens to flatterers, is like the sheep who gives milk to the wolf, or like the one who leads another by the hand then puts his foot before him to trip him. When you find that these slick merchants are praising you to the heavens, ask them out of courtesy to let you remain on earth, telling them that if you need to be praised, you will do it yourself. You can also do as a certain gentleman friend of mine did, who, after listening for a long time and with great patience to a flatterer who had praised him above the moon, finally said to him, *"I do not know what to make of these praises, for if I refuse them, I shall accuse you of flattery, and if I accept them, I shall show myself desirous of vain glory; therefore as good companions let us divide them, give me half and take the other for yourself."*

William. But in all discretion, the gentleman should not have taken half but should have given up all.

Anniball. No, with your permission, he showed great discretion in this, because flattery is always mixed with a part of the truth, it was wise to accept the truth and leave the lies to the flatterer.

William. I like your opinion about the repulse we should give to such counterfeit praises, but on this point, doubt comes to my mind. If I am moved by the goodwill I bear you and having the proper occasion, were to give you in your presence true and due praise which you have deserved for some work of yours, is it your part to reject it, or to pass it over in silence?

Anniball. That silence would be a sign of disdain or levity. I would either answer you with Christian humility, referring those praises to God as the occasion of all good, or else with moral modesty. I would seek to diminish my glory somewhat and include you or someone else in this praise. In the same way as Pyrrhus[68], the great captain, who, returning from war with a speedy and prosperous victory heard his soldiers call him a valiant eagle, replied, *"If I am an eagle, you are the cause of it, with your arms and weapons, as if they were feathers, you have sustained and supported me."* It is time to leave the conversation of the flatterers and to conclude that if someone is happy does not flatter others and does not suffer to be flattered by others; does not deceive and is not deceived; does not do harm and does not allow harm to be done to him.

William. Since the friend and the flatterer have so much conformity with each other that one can hardly distinguish one from the other, please instruct me on how I should behave, so I am not considered a flatterer.

Anniball. You must observe two things: one, never praise a man in his presence, a fault which few people can manage. Most people do not remember the words of the Greek poet, *"He who speaks ill of me behind my back, does me no harm; he who speaks well of me before me, reproaches me."* Some will think you are proud or envious if you do not praise them. The other thing to observe is that you must take another course with them, which is to imitate the dog of Egypt, who drinks from the river Nile and then runs away. You must appear to acknowledge their merits, and not speak their praises in their presence for fear that they will think you flatter them, nevertheless leaving this sweet taste in their mouth.

William. Are there any other people who are part of the rank of the tolerable, who are not desired and not avoided?

Anniball. I have already told you that the vice of flattery is not opposed to contradiction, and so I think it is good that we talk about these contentious fellows, who are obstinate in resisting the opinions of others, and will not go away until they have the last word, without weighing the antipathy or displeasure of others.

William. Although I cannot bear the qualities and company of this kind of men, I remember hearing about a noble and virtuous gentleman who gave a good account of them saying, *"They are endowed with an excellent wit, those who can maintain their private opinions against the common opinion of all, and we listen to them with more attention and admiration."* In truth, if you were to prove to me by a long discussion that the sun is brighter and warmer, I would have little interest in listening to you since you are telling me nothing that I don't already know. Oh! If you made a convincing argument that it is dark and cold, you would pique my curiosity causing me to pay attention to you. That is why a certain philosopher, hearing that there was someone who was preparing to make a speech in praise of Hercules answered, *"Why? Who discredits him?"* On the contrary, with what pleasure and admiration did we read the paradoxes of many wise and learned writers, especially the pleasant pamphlets made in praise of the plague and of French smallpox? If you answer that this belongs to a rather fantastic poet than to a serious author, I would have you consider that the philosopher Favorinus[69] is esteemed only for the fame he has won for extolling, with many and singular praises, the quartan ague (malaria), which notwithstanding, the French wish for their enemies as the greatest evil that can befall them. Therefore, I am of opinion that the most difficult things contain the most excellence and admiration. I see philosophers dispute and argue against one another and hold singular opinions far from the truth so that the gentleman of whom I have just now spoken would place these men among the desirable than among the tolerable.

Anniball. I think it is good that the people you have just named should be ranked among the desirable and commendable since they are not contentious people. Although they depart from the truth, they have some show of reason when they talk. Besides, they do not think what they say, they speak for no other purpose than to show their keen and good wit, not that they conceived such an opinion in themselves. It would be great folly to think that Favorinus was desirous of having the quartan ague and those other writers the plague. But those, whom I call contentious and overbearing, are, for the most part, gross headed fellows. There is an old saying, *"The vice of contradiction is peculiar to men of little discretion."* They oppose the truth either through ignorance or obstinacy. They are like heretics who, convinced by invincible reasons, are unwilling to yield anything but go on answering the contrary. Moreover, these fellow companions love to get along with everyone and yet always end up the worse. When they can no longer support the argument for any reason, they enter into conflict and seek to gain the upper hand by shouting, swearing, threatening, and arrogant demeanor. Sometimes they meet others of the same nature which leads them to dire debates and confrontations with each other, even for trifling matters.

Concerning what you say afterward about philosophers, I reply that it is not only appropriate and proper for them to argue but also for all others, when they reason with each other and are of contrary opinions. They deserve the highest praise of those who defend the most difficult parts and though they disagree in words, they disagree not in mutual love and goodwill, but seek the truth with one accord. Not unlike those who make rope, who, though they wind and twist one contrary to the other will still accomplish the work they set out to do. Nevertheless, disputes have their prescribed bounds and limits. Those who exceed these limits lose the name of the disputant and obtain the title of a quarrelsome professional, sometimes paying a price for being too earnest in their opposition because they have been diverted from the correct understanding of the argument. By making things too thin and fine, they quickly break down causing too much contention so that the truth is made intricate and doubtful. That is why we must call them contentious. They do not argue for the purpose of disputing or exercising their minds but out of contemptuous arrogance. They hold arguments not only repugnant to the truth, but off-key with reason.

William.   What do you think is the reason for this shortfall?

Anniball.   Marrying a mother that has two children is ignorance, self-love, and of vain persuasion. It only follows that those who know nothing believe they know everything and take their ignorance for wisdom.

William.   Indeed, the first chapter of fools is to consider their self wise.

Anniball.   You know that it is the easiest thing in the world for a man to do is deceive himself. The wise man admonishes us not to be wise in our own conceit, for such wisdom is over the top. Indeed, he who knows the most takes it upon himself the least and yields to reason. Therefore, it is no wonder that ignorant people are full of contention. We can conclude that to reason without reason is to take the trouble to make your self look bad. These quarrelsome people are mostly to be blamed even though we must pretend to bear with them.

William.   Just as you have shown how we can defend ourselves against slanderers and flatterers, show me how we should behave with these overbearing people.

Anniball.   When you find that you are getting nowhere by reasoning with your friend, and suspect there is some trouble, you should bow rather than break, yielding to his humor, except in the case where silence may be the greater offense. When a man abandons reason and allows himself to be overcome by anger, it is our duty to bear wisely with his imperfection. According to the proverb, *"Cut not the fire with iron"*, we sometimes must permit prudence to give way to temerity.

William. I know a gentleman who, if he happens to be in the company of one of these obstinate fellows would rather not quarrel with them and usually says, "*Sir, I will not argue with you about this matter since I am content it shall be as you say.*" Someone asked him one time which eye, the right or the left, was able to discern something further from the truth, he answered at once, "Whichever you please."

Anniball. Such answers, if made in a polite manner without mockery are very convenient and have enough force to make an obstinate person acknowledge their fault.

William. Do you not think we have spoken enough about this manner of men?

Anniball. I think we may couple with these, some other troublesome fellows, who offend not from ignorance but to sharpen their wits, so they can provoke others. They will make a comment on every word and lie in wait to take others on a journey with what they will say. This fault is peculiar to certain schoolmasters and other professors of learning who often shape newly discovered answers and now and then inject doubt which is enough to make a dog run a mile without looking behind him. Sometimes they meet their match and are given the respect that they deserve. Much like a poor cunning clown who served his son, who on every word would argue with him, one day only four eggs upon the dinner table. The young man, to show his wit, decided to prove that there were seven because three is contained in the number four, and four and three make seven. The father, in order to avoid an argument, took the four eggs saying, *"I will eat these and you take the other three."*

William. What remains to be said now?

Anniball. We must now speak of liars, who depart from the truth for another purpose and in another way than the contentious do. In the first place, liars are flatterers, pretenders, boasters, and vainglorious, who never cease to put forth their own praises interlacing lies among them. This is a fault that is not great and leads us to dislike them. There is nothing more repugnant than to hear someone boast about themselves.

William. They are called household witnesses who praise themselves for lack of good neighbors.

Anniball. They would do better to spend the time they waste on praising themselves or to put it more truthfully, blaming themselves, in order to obtain true praise for commendable actions, which comes only from people worthy of praise. They are so enamored with themselves that they do not notice anything of others, forgetting the sayings, *"He who washes his mouth with his own praise, soils himself with the suds that come out of it"* and *"Praise in a man's own mouth is spilled."* Just as the fault of these vain speakers is slight when it hurts nobody, it is grave and heinous when it harms others. Among the many examples that could be alleged, one cannot hide the wickedness of those who boast of their worthy conquests in the matters of love, betraying the frailty of some women to whom they promised secrecy by thousands of other false oaths.

Which afterwards the winds, disperse amid the air.

William.   The oaths of lovers have as much credit as the vows of sailors. What do you think of those who falsely boast of having had the use of a woman to whom they have never spoken to in their lives? They seek to taint her with reproach much like the false accusers of the innocent Susanna[70] once did.

Anniball.   Those who cast such slanders deserve to have the wind knocked out of them with a halter[71]. Those who lightly believe these obscene tales and tell them again deserve no less. As a result, it will not take long for an honest woman to be unjustly taken by the people for a common harlot. I leave you to think what heartache it is for her to be unjustly slandered like that. Let us conclude that all lies that are directed to the harm or dishonor of others are diabolical and detestable.

William.   I, for one, prefer to stay away from the company of those other liars, who never tell the truth, even if it doesn't hurt anyone.

Anniball.   You are right, just as someone who speaks the truth clearly shows themselves to be an honest person and of noble station. He who lies acts more like a slave; disloyal, unjust, and indiscreet person. Therefore, wise men should impress upon their hearts the saying of Pythagoras, who, when asked if men did anything to make them like God, answered that *"They spoke the truth."* If you observe the nature of liars, you will find them impudent and unashamed and that is why a philosopher said, *"Justice resembles a pure virgin, and her purity is stained by lying."* Lying is unseemly to everyone, yet it is more tolerable in one of low calling and who is driven to it by necessity. That is why, in the

Holy Scripture, a rich man who lies is severely reprimanded.

William. There are many who think they are making a name for themselves as pleasant conceited fellows by telling some monstrous and strange story. They make listeners amused or cause them to marvel, and they crave the poet's privilege to use the figure of hyperbole as they please. Such as the one, while out hunting, told the story of when he found a boar so old that was completely blind and another young boar, out of compassion, put his tail in the old boar's mouth and was leading him to food. He shot at them, cutting off the tail of the young boar which was still hanging in the mouth of the old boar. The hunter then quickly took the tail in his hand and brought the poor boar back to the city, still thinking that his companion was leading him.

Anniball. I think it was more trouble for him to tell this tale than leading the boar.

William. These people so sincerely persuade themselves to believe a lie that they would like you to believe it too, and if you don't they think you are mistreating them.

Anniball. It is good not to believe them, but they do us wrong by forcing us to believe what is false, which is nothing more than judging us and taunt us as gullible fools. In the end, they do penance for their guilt being known to manipulate and lie to others. They are never credited again, even if they tell the truth, as the following saying shows.

> *The liar is not believed, even if he tells the truth,*
> *an honest man is always believed, even if he lies.*

116

I do not deny, but it is commendable to coin a lie at some time and in some place so that it tends to some honest end.

William. I am reminded, regarding this kind of lying of a pleasant example which occurred at Court where I knew a son of a prince, about twelve years of age. His conduct and good conditions surpassed all his equals at Court, but he had a childish fault which they could not get him to stop by admonishing, rebuking, or threatening him. The young prince suffered through negligence and did not care to wipe his nose because of these constant sniffles. His governor sought to correct this problem. One day a poor old man came before this child to ask for his devotion. The old man's nose, through some disease, had become extraordinarily large, deformed, pimply, excessive, and monstrous. The child, with a certain fear mingled with compassion, was very moved, whereupon his discreet governor began to tell him that he had known this poor man for a long time and remembered having seen him in his youth with a small, well-made, and healthy nose, but after all the sniffling and filth from not wiping and keeping it clean had put him in this state. The child was so frightened by these words that he immediately began to spit, blow, and wipe his nose in such a manner that he never needed to be reminded of it again. Therefore, this lie was advantageous to the Prince and commendable to the governor.

Anniball. This is very true and just as these liars are to be praised, others are to be blamed and listed among those who are neither desirable nor avoidable. Besides, there are certain curious ones to be disapproved of, who trouble everyone by always using this word "wherefore", wanting to enter too much into other men's affairs which is perhaps a greater fault than one thinks. There is never a curious person, but who is also malicious, and moreover too talkative, playing the bearer of stories from one to another. That is why the poet blames the one who is curious about what he has nothing to do with.

William. If I remember correctly, I read about a man who, carrying a gift under his coat and being asked what he was carrying there, replied, *"Do you not see that it is hidden on purpose, lest you should know it?"*

Anniball. I remember reading the same thing and another similar story about King Antigonus[72] while passing by his army entered the tent of Antagoras[73] the Poet, having found him boiling some fish said to him, *"Do you think that Homer was busy boiling fish while he was writing the deeds of Agamemnon[74]?"* To which the poet replied, *"Do you think that Agamemnon, busy with the execution of his undertakings, was curious to know if there were any sodden fish in his camp?"* If curiosity is objectionable in worldly affairs, it is detestable in matters of religion, and therefore we are warned not to seek to know things which it is not our business to know. Now, just as the curious are neither to be desired nor avoided, we ought to take account of ambitions.

The motives of ambition

William. So your opinion is, as I see it, ambition produces negative effects?

Anniball. Why, who doesn't know that?

William. For my part, I do not see how it can do anything but good, since it awakens slumbering minds, drives away laziness and fear, awakens the mind to the understanding of commendable things and to the execution of courageous undertakings, and raises those who follow it to the highest degree of dignity and honor.

Anniball. So long as a man does not overstep these bounds, he must not be called ambitious, but courageous, for these are commendable works and virtues. The same cannot be said of those who proceed naturally from ambition, which deprives them entirely of rest, which puts no check upon their restless desires. It fills them with pensive care, blinds their understanding, and raises them up with the intention of throwing them down, breaking their necks, and driving them to destruction. It is said that Lucifer, through pride and ambition, fell from heaven wanting to command rather than to obey. Another said, *"Ambition is the cross and torment of the ambitious."* So, when I said that ambition is the cause of many cases of abuse, I did not mean those men who, knowing their own worth aspire to high enterprises and honors, which by the instinct of nature, we all covet. Honor is the reward of virtue and is considered a divine thing. I refer to the ambitious who, without taking any pains, without doing anything worthy of a noble mind, and without any foundation of reward seek the company of others and to be placed above them.

William. Those indeed are to be detested. I know some who upon entering the door or sitting down at the table put their foot in front of others and are very displeased when they usurp that foolish preeminence over them. Not knowing the place does not give or take away virtue.

Anniball. Those who do so feel that they are not highly regarded and know very well that no one will say to them, *"Please, go ahead."* But, it is true glory and a sign of great reward when this honor is given to a person without having to strive for it. It is certain that when someone lays aside all ambition and humbles himself below others, in my estimation comes from a better education. Women fall chiefly into this vanity and hence there often arises among them the best sport in the world. None of them are willing to yield their place and all are ready to take it. They occupy the way and the upper rooms as if by force. Moreover, you will often hear one of them say, *"My husband is a doctor,"* another, *"Mine is a gentleman,"* another, *"I am descended from the Trojans,"* while another boasts of her dowry and jewels and being able to buy the other out from under their own home. If husbands have these types of disputes, they are usually decided or determined by blows between them.

William. What do you think of the ambition of those men who are never cheerful or in a good mood except when they have a great host of servants at their heels? If by chance they want them and do not have them, such is their folly or fancy, that they will not leave their own home.

Anniball. This kind of ambition is common to asses that do not go forward if they have no one to follow them. Among the ambitious are the arrogant and proud whose company is distasteful and contrary to our nature, to which humanity and courtesy are most agreeable. In my opinion, such people can be compared to tyrants who do not care to be hated but feared. That is why people like this never humble themselves fearing that if they show themselves to be a good person and companion, they would become despised, and hence their reputation would be diminished. These people make a big deal about their self and swell with pride, but rest assured that their hearts are filled more with the wind than with merit.

William. Oh, how these glorious fellows are hated by the French. This is because they cannot stand the Spaniards, who are considered very proud and lofty, especially by those who do not know them well. I say this because I have been in the company of some of them who, in appearance seemed very high-minded, but in reality were very lowly.

Anniball. It may be that the Spanish do not like the French either because of their easy acquaintance and sudden familiarity. In my opinion, between these two extremes, we the Italians stand in the middle where you will see a combination of a grave kind of courtesy and courteous kind of gravity. Those whom I call proud and high-minded offend by their appearance and in their actions while standing in their expensive shoes despising everyone and expecting to be honored by all. We should not seek to live familiarly with them, but humbly honor them and offer up incense unto them, as you would at a sacred altar, so that there is no wonder if they are odious to others. This kind of man, a pleasant writer mocks, saying, *"This meat has an unpleasant taste and smells like smoke."* What I am saying is hateful to men, since God himself hates them, and who resists the proud and shows mercy to the meek and humble of heart.

William. One can say of these men, what the poet writes.

> *He falls the lowest*
> *who seeks to climb the highest.*

Anniball. Our discussion would be too long and perhaps superfluous if we were to seek out one after the other all those who are tainted with this defect and inform ourselves as to their nature and quality. For this reason, I think we should end our discussion about this point.

Wrap it up

William. There is still something that sticks in my stomach, it is your opinion that we should avoid only the infamous and those who are notoriously bad that tolerate the evil which we have mentioned here, and in my opinion, you loosen the reins of this conversation too much.

Anniball. I could answer you, according to the rules of civilized people, we ought to restrain those things which are evil and give free rein to those things which are commendable in the number we presume conversation to be. I will tell you from the way I have treated the matter it is rather restrained than otherwise. Although I have permitted you to tolerate, that is, not to seek or shun the above-mentioned people, who are many, I have not given you the liberty to seek or implore the company of others than the good, who are few in number. Whoever observes this order may accompany many by chance but few by choice. You yourself, through your affairs or other accident, will have to deal with many people. Some of them you will like much better and more willingly desire the company of one or two people whom you will have affection for because of the good parts you know to be in them. So, I conclude that the company which comes to us by chance consists of many people. That which is voluntary ought to be coveted, as it contains only a few.

William. For every one doubt you get rid of, seven appear in its place, much like the saying,

> *With each step, a new thought appears.*

Now tell me, if a harlot, or a prostitute, or some such defamed person comes into the open street or some other public place and starts talking to me, you would like me to, without allowing them to meet me, run away from them as if they were excommunicated or had the plague.

Anniball. As a private person, you should not have to pay attention to their words, but as a magistrate, it would not be amiss.

William. It is contrary to your first order if someone listens and does not flee from them. If they do not flee, they are behaving indifferently toward the intolerable and the tolerable which is also contrary to your distinction.

Anniball. If a harlot, ruffian, or other infamous person went to the Duke, your master, to ask for justice or to make some other honest request, would he drive them from his presence?

William. No.

Anniball. If they came to speak with him personally, would he send them packing out of his sight?

William. There is no doubt about it.

Anniball. By this diversity, you may know, that the intolerable are sometimes tolerable, not with respect to themselves, but on the occasion which brings them into the company of others.

William. I understand you, but other doubts arise because among these tolerable whom we have named there is a great difference in their imperfections. For the fault of a vainglorious braggart or a contentious obstructionist is far less than a pernicious flatterer or a malicious slanderer and yet you place them all in the same predicament. Besides, it seems impossible to me that someone who has one of these faults should be inclined to good rather than evil. One of these has the power to obscure and deface all the good parts that will be in them. Therefore, in my opinion, they are to be placed in the number of the intolerable.

Anniball. We have already concluded if you remember, that we must admit into our company all those who are not marked in the extreme and who are not commonly held to be defamed nor excluded from the good and honest company even though they are sprinkled with some imperfections.

To satisfy you, how may men of diverse nations did you know while at the court of France?

William. I knew there were many besides the French, Spanish, English, Flemish, Almans, Scots, and Italians.

Anniball. Which of them have you talked to most often and willingly?

William. You probably think I chose the company of Italians.

Anniball. Which Italians?

William. The Lombards.

Anniball. Among the Lombards, what was your choice?

William. Those of my own country.

Anniball. And of those, which did you like best?

William. Those who were most agreeable to my mind, as the saying goes, *"Every like desires its like."*

Anniball. The same is true that we naturally abhor things that differ from our nature. Hence, it follows that the one who, is well-disposed, cannot bear one who is ill-disposed. Someone who is dull cannot abide with one who has a sharp wit; and on the contrary, the merry like the merry, and the sad like the sad. Therefore, we must consider that nature has given us two people, one is common to all men, inasmuch as they are partakers of reason and more excellent than beasts. The other is proper to everyone because of the difference which is seen in the countenance and appearance of the body and in the diversity of the minds which each tends and inclines not only to some good, but also to some evil. In this way, you see that one offends by arrogance, another by obstinacy, misreporting, flattery, covetousness, vaingloriousness and you must think that there is no one in whom there is not some fault or imperfection either greater or lesser than that which is in us. We can find neither friends nor relatives who are in every respect agreeable to our disposition and nature. We must get used to bearing the imperfections of others and as the saying goes, *"We must love a friend with his imperfection."* Since perfect and virtuous men are rare in the world, with whom we could live according to our desires, we must not refuse the company of anyone if they have in them some token of virtue and goodness. To be acceptable in the company of others we must put aside our own decorum and manners and clothe ourselves in the conditions of others while imitating them as far as reason will permit. In some cases, as far as honesty and virtue are concerned, we should always be one and the same. As far as the diversity of the people we will have to deal with, we should become another person, according to the old saying, *"The heart altogether different and the face entirely like the people."* When someone is not willing to do this they will be driven to curse the conversation and pray to God like the snail, as stated in the fable[75], in order to avoid bad neighbors and bad company, allow him to be able to carry his house with him. We should not persuade ourselves that we are free from fault. I am sure that if I refused the company of a contentious fellow, perhaps he would refuse mine for some greater imperfection. Therefore, I am of the opinion that without looking too precisely at any one fault we must admit the company of all those who in the rest of their works and actions walk upright. It is okay, at times, to act as if we did not see their faults and had a good opinion of them. In this respect, I recall the actions of the Duke of Nevers who, making a feast in this city, entrusted the charge of inviting the ladies to a young man who had the reputation of being very vicious and wicked. The citizens were very displeased since his Excellency was aware of the young man's qualities. While talking with each other, some ladies began to play a sort of game, at which time one of them joined in asking the Duke why, since there were so many young gentlemen of great wisdom and good conduct in the city he allowed them to be invited to the feast by a dishonest and ill-disposed person. The Duke replied that he was sure that he and the good ones should always get along and therefore deemed it necessary to win the goodwill of the bad ones by some means.

William. I understand that he wanted to imitate the one who lights his candle before the image of the devil. However, in my opinion, to favor the bad is to offend the good and I wonder how a prince of such discreet judgment could make such a poor choice. I think he did it because, not having long to stay there, he sought in every way to have everyone think well of him after his departure and like the sun, he wanted to spread the rays of his goodness on all sorts of people. I assure you he would not have made such a choice in his own country, where he does not have to learn to distinguish the qualities of his subjects to raise up the good and throw down the bad.

Anniball. I believe that it is necessary to do so, but I do not think he did for the reason you speak of. For wise men of good judgment, they do not care if bad people love them. They know when they are well thought of by the bad, the opposite is true by the good.

William. I am persuaded that all men of understanding strive hard to obtain goodwill, even the most wicked. For my part, I do not wish to have the ill will of any, whether good or bad. I pray to God to give me the grace to be able to fully satisfy all kinds of people.

Anniball. Then you should have a special privilege over all other men. But remember the old proverb that Jupiter himself does not please everybody. I have never yet known a man so good and virtuous who has not been subject to the malice and slander of some. I tell you resolutely that not caring what is said about you and your desire to not please anyone will only play an arrogant and proud part. You will become too scrupulous and will never be cured of your disease if you think to stop every mouth that would eat away at your heart, as they say. Take heed to only please the good and never mind what the wicked say or think of you because their insults cannot hurt virtue and innocence. Know that the divine philosopher does not want us to care about what the multitude say about us, only what a wise and discreet man gives.

William. Do you not see that when a strange gentleman comes to visit us in our house, how careful we are to see that his servants are well treated? There is no other reason to fear that they will later make some bad report about us. We are safe when the masters are content with the entertainment we give them.

Anniball. I think that servants, being naturally talkative and full of tongue, do it in hope that they will bring out our courtesy, than from fear that they may find fault with our eagerness. Our goodwill and courtesy cannot be fully shown on our part, nor gratefully accepted from the head if they do not extend to the members. You know that there are certain masters of such a nature who love the comfort and good use of their servants more than themselves. Therefore, all good cheer that is bestowed upon them is in respect towards their masters. Be that as it may, I am resolved in this that we ought to do well for the love of virtue and not for fear of a bad report.

William. There are some who act well, not for the love of virtue or for the fear of infamy, but for heroism. Such as those who, in fairs and markets show great liberality in giving gifts to women only to return home and complain about it and deprive their poor servants of their wages.

Anniball. Such liberality is like the match of a candle which must fail immediately so that its renown lasts no longer than the fair. They may well be compared to certain little bugs called mayflies which are bred by the river of Hypanis in Scythia whose life lasts but a day. I think that these men make a profession out of losing their credit at home in order to get it abroad. However, when the foul breath comes from the stomach it is no great effort to put something sweet in the mouth in order to leave a pleasant smell in it. Eventually, you will taste the vessel because the bad taste will rise. They may think they are treated well enough to be put in the rank of the tolerable ones.

William, I have been so carried away by the pleasantness of our conversation that I did not notice how much time had passed that should have been devoted to visiting with my patients. Since we agree that conversation is profitable and necessary, that men of an evil nature are avoided, those who are devoted to good more than bad are to be tolerated, and the good and virtuous are to be desired. I will for the present take my leave of you and come back tomorrow, if you please, to talk another hour about the civil and commendable manners of conversation according to our determination.

William. Your return will be more grateful to me than your departure and I assure you that this little space between us will seem long to me. Go in God's name and return afterward to redouble my comfort.

Anniball. The comfort will be mutual, for our love is mutual. Farewell.

The end of the first Book.

Letter to the Lady Norrice

To the honorable, and his very good Lady,
The Lady Norrice,
George Pettie wishes contentment
in all things.

Good Madam, the strength of virtue is such that it acquires in those who are related to it the good will of those who are strangers to it. My own make me dutifully affectionate to your Ladyship, which is no stranger to you or unaware of your noble and virtuous disposition. As a sign of my duty and affection I present to you the first sight of my translation. I humbly entrust it to your honorable protection, knowing that no one will more willingly undertake the defense of learning. Therefore, those who are induced with singular wit and learning and do not think anyone is more worthy to receive its first fruits, then those that are particularly conducive to learning.

I will not enter the vast field of your virtues because I know you enjoy doing well, more than hearing well, and for this the right coral does not need colors, or the beautiful marble painting, or my pen. My words cannot procure more honor to your name than it has already obtained, partly from your own actions, and partly from the renowned deeds of your sons; noble gentlemen provided with such wisdom, discretion and sufficiency in every way, that our Prince and our country cannot spare their good service. Some are induced with such valor that our country is too small to contain the greatness of their minds, some with such manly ability even in their younger years, who assisted our country recently in no small steed in suppressing and subduing our rebellious enemies. Should some of them like Alexander the Great seek newer Countries and newer Worlds to show their valor; nevertheless they remain very ready to render service in the country, whenever it will please our Prince to command their return. God wishes that he could please his Majesty with the speed of commanding him. These rare jewels are well worth being worn as it is necessary to have such worthy captains in these dangerous times. Their bravery is sufficiently known by all men and whose fidelity may be sufficiently guaranteed to your Highness, by the good and trustworthy service of their noble father, my Lord Norrice, both within and outside the Kingdom, and of their worthy grandfather, my Lord Williams, both before her Majesty came to the Crown, and after.

By the rare virtue they have shown and the faithful service they have rendered, whose credit is so great and name so renowned it will never die while the Low Countries, while Macklin, while Stenewike, no, not while the world stands. If any name within these years of late, their valiant deeds have won an honor to

England (without exception), it is the name of the Norrice's. And if some parents in England can be happy with their children, that is my Lord Norrice and your Ladyship. You can be compared with Olympias[76] for her Alexander, with Hecuba[77] for her Hector, with Thetis[78] for her Achilles. And if you are asked where your jewels are, you can point with Cornelia[79] to your children, and you may point out that rare jewel that you continually have on you, which in both virtue and beauty exceeds the richest diamond and the most precious pearl that exists.

It appears that I am entering into an affair without end, so I will stay at the beginning. I humbly ask you to accept in good part this little proof of my good will, and that you are assured of my readiness to serve you in greater matters when you are pleased to employ me.

From my lodging, this February 6th, 1581.

Your Ladyships readily to command,

George Pettie.

Note from George Pettie

Having (kind Readers) by reason of an insignificant work[80] of mine (because of its lightness or at least because of its author, flew abroad before I knew of it) had obtained such fame as the one who burned the Temple of Dianae[81]. I thought it best to buy myself a little better fame by some better work and to counter my former vanity with a certain formal graveness. Even though I know fame is dangerous because if it is good, envy follows it and if it is ill, shame accompanies it. Seeing the work, it cannot be revoked, and having already past the peeks in a dangerous conflict without wounding my honor (such was your courtesy) I have no doubt now, but to escape some heartbreaking blow in a light skirmish, without even enduring the discharge of their arms. The men who will criticize me harshly would rather be counted as friendly foes than deadly enemies. Those who will never dislike me or the matter that I will present to you, but who would have, as it were, to my credit, think it convenient that I (whose profession should chiefly be weapons) spend time writing books or publishing them.

People who dislike studying or learning in their youth can be referred to as a Freshwater Soldier.[82] They think that in war it is only the body that must bear the worst part, not knowing that the body is governed by the mind. In all doubts and dangerous matters, it is the mind alone that is the man. Having shown elsewhere how necessary learning is for soldiers, I only warn that if in England we frame ourselves only for war, we are not a very well-oiled machine. We will not be able to prevent ourselves from rusting; with such a long continuance of peace… it has pleased God to bless us. Those who do not like to publish the fruits of his learning are some curious gentlemen. They think it is more commendable in a gentleman to cover up his art and skill in everything, as they seem to do all things from the understanding of their own mother. They do not consider that we do not deserve praise for what God or Nature has given us, but only for what we purchase from our own industry. If you dare reason with them they will, at the drop of a hat, protest that they are not scholars, despite having spent all their time studying. Why gentlemen, is it a shame to show that you are educated? Is it a shame not to be? In many things, nothing is as good as learning. You desire to hide your education, which is your best quality, yet you are afraid to show what you are. Unfortunately, you will be nothing more than an unkind gentleman if you are not scholarly.

You will do your Prince a simple service and stand for

your country but on a slender path. You will bring yourself limited advancement if you are not scholarly. Can you advise your Prince wisely to foresee threats with providence and govern affairs of the state with discretion without learning? No, the experience must be your guide, which will only be a blind one. It must be your Schoolmaster, but you will find it dangerous. To go lower, can you converse with strangers and ask about the state of foreign countries, entertain ambassadors, without being scholars? No, unless it is with dumb shows and signs. Recently a nice gentleman who could have spoken, if he had been entrusted, however, being among others was ordered to ride to meet an ambassador on his way to Court. On his return, a nobleman asked him happily what he said to the Ambassador when he met him. "Nothing", he said, "but kissed my horse's mane, and came my way."

Putting it mildly, can you tell your mistress a good story or delight her with a nice figure of speech, being uneducated? No, it needs to be totally unsavory or seasoned with salt from others. Do you think it is more embarrassing to you if you show that you have a story of your own or that she knows you stole it from others?

You know Caesar was a brave gentleman and a Scholar who wrote books that were published. Marcus Aurelius[83] was an emperor, scholar, and started scholarly works. Therefore, (Gentlemen) never deny that you are Scholars, never be ashamed to show your knowledge; confess it, profess it, embrace it, and honor it. It is your education that honors you and what makes you gentlemen. Mark my words, if there is anyone anywhere, who seeks to climb or benefit himself through flattery, corruption, slavery, or wickedness, I dare to assure you that he is completely ignorant. Since having no good part in him or good gifts which would benefit him, he flies toward those sinister aspects of himself as his safest course. You can see that it is learning that makes the accomplished gentleman and the lack of education that stains him. Neither the kindness of the character or the gaiety of the clothes or any of the external ornamentation can be compared to the features of knowledge. Though a man may display his pridefulness in the best way and not take it lightly, he will never be counted among the wise or ever be presented in the role of a just and sufficient gentleman. I hope this satisfies those who do not like the gentlemen that publish the fruits of their study, especially seeing that learning is advanced, and large numbers are gratified and profitable. The only way to earn immortality is to do things worthy of writing or write about things worthy of being read. If they object to those that search for immortality as a sign of vanity, answer them plainly and graciously that those who do not go beyond praise will never do anything worthy of acclaim.

There are some who will enjoy my work because I write in English and these travelers are very nice. Some go home with such queasy stomachs that nothing is going to appease them except in French, Italian, or Spanish. Even though someone's work will be respectfully written in one of those languages, and finely translated into our language, they will not adhere far from preferring the original before the translation. The cause in part is that they cannot catch flaws in a foreign language as in their own. This makes them think that the work is current, which is of course, and in part, because strange things delight them more so than what they are used to on a daily basis. They do not consider the benefit of reading things in their own language, where they will understand the material much sooner. If they read it in a foreign language, they will not be able to speak, discuss, or write, nor indict properly, decently, finely, or wisely. The worst thing is that they think it is impossible to translate the material into our language because they consider it barren, barbaric, and unworthy (or undeserving) of interpretation. This is regrettable, as I have heard some of them report abroad that our country is barbarous, our manners rude, and our people uncivil. I have stood with them in comparing other countries with ours and pointed my finger to many gross cases of abuse, used in places where we have been. When for no reason they have been able to defend their criticisms, they have shrunk on their necks[84] and told me it was the fashion of the country. They did not consider that the manner and fashions of each country are the only things that make it counted as barbarous or civil, good or bad.

I am convinced that those who know and love our country will report it as the most civilized country in the world. If foreigners think it otherwise, the disorders of those travelers abroad are the main cause of it. Speaking only of the lighter ones who envy, deprave, mock, quarrel, and fight in the open street. With embarrassment, I have often beheld in Paris, contempt for their countries fashions, their apish imitation of the outlandish asses in their gestures, behaviors, and clothes, are the only causes that make foreigners consider our country and our people barbarians. It is well-known that we live with laws equally orderly, in ways equally decent, in appearance as pleasant, in the diet as delicately, in accommodation as curious, in buildings as lavishly, in all things as abundantly, and in every way as civilly, like any nation under heaven. Because of the barbarity of our language, I must say that it is much worse for them. For some curious fellows, if one dares to derive a word from Latin which is insolent to their ears (as perhaps they will take that phrase to be), they immediately make a joke and call it an Inkhorn[85] term. For my part, I use those words as little as possible. I do not know of any reason why I should not use them and I find it a fault in myself if I do not. In fact, it is the easiest way to enrich our language and make it copious. It is the path that all languages have taken to enrich themselves. Remove the Latin words from the Spanish language and it will be as barren as most of their country. Take them from Italian and somehow you take away the whole tongue. Take them away from French and you will spoil its grace. Remove Greek words derived from Latin itself and it won't be as fluid and flourishing as it is. I marvel at how our English language has evolved because it does not borrow from Latin as well as other languages. If it has been borrowed, it is only in recent times because it is not well-known to all men how many words we have taken within the past few years. If they were all counted, they would be known as Inkhorn terms. I do not know how we could say anything without blackening our mouths with ink. What word can be *plain* other than the word *plain*, and yet what can come closer to Latin? What more *manifest*, than *manifest*, and yet in a manner Latin? What more a *commune* than *rare*, or less *rare* than a *commune*, and yet both come from Latin? But you will say prolonged usage has made these words current. Why can't we use these words so much that we will now conclude them as the norm? Why should we not do as much for posterity as we have received from the past? If something is bad by itself, I do not see how its age can make it good, and if it is good by itself, I do not see how its newness can make it nothing. Therefore, those words that you confess by use are made to be good, are good the first time they are uttered and should not be mocked or despised.

No matter how little you deal with your language, no matter how barbarous you count it, how little you consider it, I would still dare to undertake (if I were provided with the education) to write in it as copiously for variety, compendiously for brevity, as choicely for words, as pithily for sentences, as pleasantly for figures, and in every way as eloquent as any writer should do in any vulgar language. Having thus satisfied (as I hope) my curious enemies, I yearn for the goodwill of my courteous friends, hoping kind reader that you will accept in good part this, my labor. If you happen to like it, I will count my gains greatly, if not, I must consider my loss but slight, since doing it prevented me from idleness, something so dangerous for young gentlemen, that I wish everyone, above all, to avoid it. So, fare you well, from my Lodging near Paules.

Yours to employ

George Pettie.

Index

A

Abraham, 18

Academy of the Illustrati, 43

Achilles, 8, 137

Adam, 26

Aesculapius, 8

Aesop, 57

Alcibiades, 75

Alemanni, 44

Alexander, 45, 89, 92, 97, 136, 137

Almans, 127

Amphion, 19

antiphrasis, 81

Apelles, 42

Archytas of Tarentum, 33

Aristotle, 45

Artisans, 18

Athenian, 12

Atlas, 53

Augustus, 86, 89

B

Bartholomew Young, iii

Boccaccio, 66, 67

Brescia, iii

C

Caesar, 141

Carneades, 105

Casal, 43

Casale, ii

Catholic, 1

Charybdis, 20

Christ, 19, 26, 40, 68, 69

Christian, 1, 5, 25, 70, 108

Christians, 24, 46

Cinganes, 73

Cornelia, 137

corselet, 39

courtier, 36, 68, 70

Courtier, 23

courtiers, 14

Crates, 48

Cretans, 36

D

Dante, 16
Demosthenes, 93
Diogenes, 21, 28, 57, 73
Dionysius, 92
Dissemblers, 80
Domitian, 97
Duke of Nevers, 1, 129

E

Egypt, 108
Elijah, 18
Emperor Domitian, 55
Emperor Sigismund, 106
Endymion, 53
England, 137, 140
English, i, ii, iii, iv, 127, 142, 144
Epicurus, 46
Europe, 8

F

Favorinus, 110
Flemish, 127
four humors, 65
France, 1, 2, 6, 8, 72, 127
Frances Pugiella, 64
French, ii, iii, 14, 72, 94, 110, 121,
    122, 127, 142, 144
Freshwater Soldier, 140

G

Galba, 66
George Pettie, i, iii, iv, 135, 137,
    139, 145
Germans, 14
God, 5, 11, 12, 18, 19, 24, 25, 33,
    34, 40, 42, 48, 52, 54, 68, 69,
    70, 90, 97, 106, 108, 115, 122,
    129, 130, 133, 136, 140
Greek, iii, 85, 108, 144
Greeks, 62, 74

H

harquebus, 39
Hector, 137
Hecuba, 137
Hellebore, 48
Hercules, 61, 109
Homer, 35, 118
Horace, 35, 68
Hypanis, 132

I

Inkhorn, 144
Inquisition, 46
Isaac, 18
Italian, ii, iii, iv, 142, 144
Italians, 74, 122, 127, 128
Italy, ii, iii, 1, 2, 6, 43, 74

J

Jacob, 18
Jeremiah, 18
Jews, 14, 71
John the Baptist, 19
Judas, 106
Juno, 83
Jupiter, 42, 53, 83, 97, 131

K

King Antigonus, 118
King Charles IX, 1

L

Latin, 40, 144
Latins, 62
Lombards, 128
Lombardy, 74
Lord Cesar Genzaga, 43
Lord Norrice, 136, 137
Lord Williams, 136
Louis Gonzaga, 1

Index

Lucifer, 120

M

Macklin, 136
Madame Marguerite Stanga, 56
Mantua, 43
Marcus Aurelius, 141
Mariners, 64
Master Anniball Magnocavalli,
    2, 5
Master Guazzo, 5, 82
Masters of Eloquence, 80
melancholy, 6, 7, 10, 11, 34
Mercury, 19
Mermaids, 57
Montferrat, ii
Montserrat, 74
Moses, 18
Mount Caucasus, 53

N

Nicesias, 92
Nile, 109

O

Oedipus, 51
Olympias, 137
Orpheus, 19

P

Padua, 14
Paris, 6, 143
Pavia, 43
Petrarch, 23, 32, 35
Phoenix, 65
Piedmont, 72
Pittacus, 101
Po, 71, 74
Princess Eleanor of Austria, 2
Prometheus, 53
proverbs, iii, 17, 45

purgations, 2
Pythagoras, 21, 115

Q

Quartan ague, 110

R

rhetoricians, 80
Roman, iii, 74
Rome, 32, 75, 86

S

Saint Ambrose, 75
Saint-Quentin, 1
Saluce, 1
Saturn, 19
Scipio, 54
Scots, 127
Scylla, 20
sententious, 85
Sir Edward Sullivan, ii
Spaniards, 14, 121
Spanish, 122, 127, 142, 144
Stefano Guazo, ii
Stenewike, 136
Stoics, 33
Susanna, 115

T

Tanaro, 74
Temple of Dianae, 139
The Civil Conversation, i, ii
The Lady Norrice, 135
Themistocles, 93
Thetis, 137
Tortoise to enchantment, 7
Trojans, 121
Tudor, i, ii
Turks, 71
Tuscan, 35, 74
Tuscany, 35, 40

U

Ulysses, 31, 57

V

Venice, 14

Vida, 23, 32

Virgil, 35

W

William Guazzo, 5

William Shakespeare, ii

Bibliography

Guazzo, Stefano. The Civile Conversation. Translated by Pettie, George. First Volume. New York, New York: AMS Press, Inc., 1925.

Guazzo, Stefano. La Civil Conversatione. First Volume. Brescia, Italy: Appresso Tomaso Bozzola, 1574.

"Wikipedia." Wikipedia. www.wikipedia.org. https://www.wikipedia.org/.

"Dictionary By Merriam-Webster: America's Most-trusted Online Dictionary." Dictionary by Merriam-Webster: America's most-trusted online dictionary. www.merriam-webster.com. https://www.merriam-webster.com/.

"Thesaurus By Merriam-Webster." Thesaurus by Merriam-Webster: More Than Synonyms and Antonyms. www.merriam-webster.com. https://www.merriam-webster.com/thesaurus.

Notes

¹ The **Battle of Saint-Quentin** of 1557 was a decisive engagement, during the Italian War of 1551-1559, between the Kingdom of France and the Habsburg empire, at Saint-Quentin in Picardy. A Habsburg Spanish force under Duke Emmanuel Philibert of Savoy defeated a French army under the command of Duke Louis Gonzaga and Duke Anne de Montmorency.

² **Purgation** is vigorous evacuation of the bowels (as from the action of a cathartic or an infectious agent).

³ **Melancholy** is a concept found throughout ancient, medieval, and pre-modern medicine in Europe that describes a condition characterized by markedly depressed mood, bodily complaints, and sometimes hallucinations and delusions.

⁴ **Zeus and the Tortoise** appears among Aesop's Fables and explains how the tortoise got her shell. It is

numbered 106 in the Perry Index. From it derives the proverbial sentiment that 'There's no place like home'. The fable tells how the king of the gods invited all the animals to his wedding but the tortoise never arrived. When asked why, her excuse was that she preferred her own home, so Zeus made her carry her house about forever after.

[5] **Aesculapius** - the ancient Roman god of medicine, whose staff with a snake curled around it is commonly used as a symbol of medicine.

[6] **Courtier** - a person who attends a royal court as a companion or adviser to the king or queen.

[7] **Dante's Divine Comedy, Inferno** – Canto X1:89-90

> *You content me so, when you resolve,*
> *that doubting pleases me no less than knowing!*

[8] Greek and Roman Mythology - Greek deities were adopted by the Romans. The name in parenthesis is the Roman equivalent.

- **Amphion:** Musician; husband of Niobe; charmed stones to build fortifications for Thebes.

- **Cronus (Saturn):** Titan; god of harvests; son of Uranus and Gaea; dethroned by his son Zeus.

- **Hermes (Mercury):** God of physicians and thieves; messenger of gods; son of Zeus and Maia.

- **Orpheus:** Famed musician; son of Apollo and Muse Calliope; husband of Eurydice.

[9] The reference between **Scylla and Charybdis** is an

idiom deriving from Greek mythology, which has been associated with the proverbial advice "to choose the lesser of two evils" or "between a rock and a hard place".

[10] Diogenes also known as **Diogenes the Cynic** was a Greek philosopher and one of the founders of **Cynic** philosophy. He was born in Sinope, an Ionian colony on the Black Sea coast of modern-day Turkey, in 412 or 404 BC and died at Corinth in 323 BC.

[11] **Pythagoras** (c. 570 – c. 495 BC) was an ancient Ionian Greek philosopher and the founder of Pythagoreanism.

[12] **Francesco Petrarch** (20 July 1304 – 18/19 July 1374) commonly anglicized as **Petrarch** was a scholar and poet of early Renaissance, and one of the earliest humanists.

[13] **Marco Girolamo Vida** or **Marcus Hieronymus Vida** (1485 – September 27, 1566) was an Italian humanist, bishop and poet. Published in Cremona in 1535 The *Christiad,* an epic poem in six cantos on the life of Jesus Christ.

[14] The **Parable of the Hidden Treasure** is a well known parable of Jesus which appears in Matthew 13:44, and illustrates the great value of the Kingdom of Heaven.

[15] **Ulysses** is the Latin variant of **Odysseus,** the legendary Greek king of Ithaca and the hero of Homer's epic poem the *Odyssey*. He also plays a key role in Homer's *Iliad* and other works during that same time.

[16] **Stoics** are members of the ancient school of *Hellenistic philosophy* (Western and ancient Greek philosophy

during the Hellenistic period, 323 BC to 31BC) founded by *Zeno of Citium* in Athens in the early 3rd century BC. It is a philosophy of personal ethics informed by its system of logic and its views on the natural world.

17 **Archytas** was an Ancient Greek philosopher, mathematician, astronomer, statesman, and strategist. He was a scientist of the Pythagorean school and famous for being the reputed founder of mathematical mechanics, as well as a good friend of Plato.

18 **Francesco Petrarch** (20 July 1304 – 18/19 July 1374) – from his poetry: . . . The senses reign, and reason now is dead; from one pleasing desire comes another. Virtue, honor, beauty, gracious bearing, sweet words...

19 **Quintus Horatius Flaccus** (8 December 65 to 27 November 8 BC), known in the English-speaking world as **Horace**, was the leading Roman lyric poet during the time of Augustus (also known as Octavian).

20 **Homer** was the author of the Iliad and the Odyssey, the two epic poems that are the foundational works of ancient Greek literature.

21 **Publius Vergilius Maro** (15 October 70 BC to 21 September 19 BC), usually called **Virgil** or **Vergil** in English, was an ancient Roman poet of the Augustan period. He composed three of the most famous poems in Latin literature: the Eclogues (or *Bucolics*), the Georgics, and the epic Aeneid.

22 **Cretan** - a native or inhabitant of the Greek island of Crete.

23 **Corselet** - a piece of armor covering the trunk.

[24] **Harquebus** - an early type of portable gun supported on a tripod or a forked rest.

[25] **Jupiter** is the king of the gods in Roman mythology. He was the god of the sky and thunder. He is also known as Zeus in Greek mythology.

[26] **Apelles of Kos** (4th century BC) was a renowned painter of ancient Greece.

[27] The **University of Mantua**, located in Mantua, Lombardy, Italy. 1584–1630.

[28] **Duke Ferdinando Gonzaga**, a prince savant who debated Galileo, as he made his families dreams a reality. Ferdinando negotiated with the Jesuits, recruited professors, and financed the University of Mantua.

[29] The **University of Pavia** is a university located in Pavia, Lombardy, Italy. There was evidence of teaching as early as 1361, making it one of the oldest universities in the world.

[30] The **Alemanni** (also known as the Alamanni and the Alamans, meaning "All Men" or "Men United") were a confederacy of Germanic-speaking people who occupied the regions south of the Main and east of the Rhine rivers in present-day Germany.

[31] **Proverbs 13:20** - Walk with the wise and become wise, for a companion of fools suffers harm.

[32] **Ecclesiastes 13:1** - If you touch tar, it will stick to you, and if you keep company with arrogant people, you will come to be just like them.

[33] **Epicurus** (341–270 BC) was an ancient Greek

Philosopher and sage who founded Epicureanism, a highly influential school of philosophy. **Epicureanism** is a system of philosophy founded around 307 BC. It was originally a challenge to Platonism and later became a main opponent of Stoicism.

[34] **Crates** (c. 365 – c. 285 BC) of Thebes was a Greek Cynic philosopher, the principal pupil of Diogenes of Sinope, and the husband of Hipparchia of Maroneia who lived in the same manner as him. Crates gave away his money to live a life of poverty on the streets of Athens. Respected by the people of Athens, he is remembered for being the teacher of Zeno of Citium, the founder of Stoicism. Various fragments of Crates' teachings survive, including his description of the ideal Cynic state.

[35] **Hellebore** gets its common name, **Lenten rose**, from the rose-like flowers that appear in early spring around the Christian observance of Lent. Many hellebore species are poisonous.

[36] **Oedipus** was a mythical Greek king of Thebes. A tragic hero in Greek mythology, Oedipus accidentally fulfilled a prophecy that he would end up killing his father and marrying his mother, thereby bringing disaster to his city and family. Oedipus, a great and noble king was flawed **by his hubris, or spiritual pride.**

[37] **Ecclesiastes 4:10** - *For if they fall, one will lift up his fellow. But woe to him who is alone when he falls and has not another to lift him up!*

[38] **Prometheus** is the Titan god of fire. He is credited with the creation of humanity from clay, and of defying

the gods by stealing fire and giving it to humanity. As a consequence of the theft Zeus sentenced him to eternal torment for his transgression.

[39] **Endymion**, in Greek mythology, was an Aeolian shepherd, hunter, or king who was said to rule and live at Olympia in Elis. He was an astronomer and was the first human to observe the movements of the moon.

[40] **Emperor Domitian** (was Roman emperor from 81 to 96. He was the son of Vespian and the younger brother of Titus, his two predecessors on the throne, and the last member of the Flavian dynasty. During his reign, the authoritarian nature of his rule put him at sharp odds with the Senate, whose powers he drastically curtailed. Domitian was a man both physically and intellectually lazy.

[41] **Proverbs 1:17** - Surely in vain the net is spread in the sight of any bird.

[42] **Yeoman** was first documented in mid-14th-century England, referring to the middle ranks of servants in an English royal or noble household.

[43] The **four humors** were, essentially, seen as the four basic elements which made up the human body. These were: **blood, yellow bile, black bile and phlegm**. Each humor was associated with a different element, season, organ, temperament and, importantly, different qualities.

[44] **Servius Galba** (24 December 3 BC – 15 January AD 69) was a Roman emperor who ruled from AD 68 to 69. He was the first emperor in the Year of the Four Emperors and assumed the position following emperor

Nero's suicide. Prior to becoming emperor, he was named **Lucius Livius Ocella Sulpicius Galba**. His physical weakness and general apathy led to him being selected-over by favorites.

[45] **Quintus Horatius Flaccus** (8 December 65[1] – 27 November 8 BC), *see note 19*. The rhetorician Quintilian regarded his Odes as just about the only Latin lyrics worth reading: "He can be lofty sometimes, yet he is also full of charm and grace, versatile in his figures, and felicitously daring in his choice of words." The saying comes from **Horace's** Poem: **Morale Decadence** - Translated by A.S. Kline 2003 from the original Latin.

> *Worse than our grandparents' generation,*
> *Our parents' then produced us,*
> *even worse,*
> *and soon to bear still more sinful children.*

[46] **Usury**: the illegal action or practice of lending money at unreasonably high rates of interest.

[47] **Cinganes** - one of the names applied to the gypsies in the east, which has passed into various European languages (*e.g.*, Hungarian *Czigány*, French *Tsigane*, Italian *Zingari*, and German *Zigeuner*) and appears in Turkish as *Cingene*. The origin of the name is uncertain.

[48] **Alcibiades, son of Cleinias** (c. 450–404 BC), from the outskirts of Scambonidae, was a prominent Athenian statesman, orator, and general. He was the last famous member of his mother's aristocratic family, the Alcmaeonidae, which fell from prominence after the Peloponnesian War. He played a major role in the

160

second half of that conflict as a strategic advisor, military commander, and politician.

[49] **Ambrose of Milan** (c. 340 – 397), venerated as **Saint Ambrose**, was the Bishop of Milan, a theologian, and one of the most influential ecclesiastical figures of the 4th century. His most notable quote:

> *When in Rome, live as the Romans do;*
> *when elsewhere, live as they live elsewhere.*

[50] **Cur** is usually used to describe a mongrel dog particularly of aggressive or unfriendly nature.

[51] **Biters** - to respond to a comment in an angry or reproachful way.

[52] **Antiphrasis** is the usually ironic or humorous use of words in senses opposite to the generally accepted meanings (as in "this giant of 3 feet 4 inches").

[53] **Coiner** is a person who coins money, in particular a maker of counterfeit coins.

[54] **Juno** was an ancient Roman goddess, the protector and special counselor of the state. She was equated to Hera, queen of the gods in Greek mythology. A daughter of Saturn, she was the wife of Jupiter.

[55] **Sententious** - marked by or given to preaching moral values.

[56] Attributed to **Aesop's Fables**, a collection of fables credited to **Aesop**, a slave and storyteller believed to have lived in ancient Greece between 620 and 564 BC.

[57] **Nicesias** a flatterer of Alexander king of Epirus, 3rd century BC.

[58] **Dionysius I** or **Dionysius the Elder** (c.432-367 BC) was a Greek tyrant of Syracuse. He was regarded by the ancients as an example of the worst kind of despot—cruel, suspicious and vindictive.

[59] **Themistocles** (c. 524–459 BC) was an Athenian politician and general.

[60] **Demosthenes** (384 – 12 October 322 BC) was a Greek statesman and orator of ancient Athens.

[61] **Ruffs** served as changeable pieces of cloth that could themselves be laundered separately while keeping the wearer's doublet or gown from becoming soiled at the neckline. The stiffness of the garment forced upright posture, and their impracticality led them to become a symbol of wealth and status.

[62] **Seek knots in bulrushes** - To engage in a futile task; to try to find problems where none exist. A bulrush is a grassy plant that is not prone to knots.

[63] **Domitian** (24 October 51 – 18 September 96) was Roman emperor from 81 to 96. He was the son of Vespasian and the younger brother of Titus, his two predecessors on the throne, and the last member of the Flavian dynasty. During his reign, the authoritarian nature of his rule put him at sharp odds with the Senate, whose powers he drastically curtailed.

[64] **Flouter** is someone who ignores another in a disrespectful manner.

[65] **Pittacus** (c. 640 – 568 BC) was an ancient Mytilenean

military general and one of the Seven Sages of Greece.

[66] **Carneades** (214–129/8 BC) was a member and eventually scholarch or head of the Academy, the philosophical school founded by Plato, for part of its skeptical phase. He is credited by ancient tradition with founding the New or Third Academy and defended a form of probabilism in epistemology.

[67] **Sigismund** of Bohemia (15 February 1368 – 9 December 1437), also known as Sigismund of Luxembourg, was prince-elector of Brandenburg from 1378 until 1388 and from 1411 until 1415, king of Hungary and Croatia from 1387, king of Germany from 1411, king of Bohemia from 1419, king of Italy from 1431, and Holy Roman Emperor from 1433 until 1437, and the last male member of the House of Luxembourg.

[68] **Pyrrhus** (319/318–272 BC) was a Greek king and statesman of the Hellenistic period. He was king of the Greek tribe of Molossians, of the royal Aeacid house, and later he became king (Malalas also called him toparch) of Epirus. He was one of the strongest opponents of early Rome, and regarded as one of the greatest generals of antiquity. Several of his victorious battles caused him unacceptably heavy losses, from which the term "Pyrrhic victory" was coined.

[69] **Favorinus** of Arelate (c. 80 – c. 160 AD) was an intersex Roman sophist and Academic Skeptic philosopher who flourished during the reign of Hadrian and the Second Sophistic.

[70] **Susanna,** also called **Susanna and the Elders**, is a narrative included in the Book of Daniel (as chapter 13)

by the Roman Catholic and Eastern Orthodox Church.

71 A **halter** or **head collar** is headgear that is used to lead or tie up livestock and, occasionally, other animals; it fits behind the ears (behind the poll), and around the muzzle.

72 **Antigonus** I Monophthalmus (Antigonus the One-Eyed, 382 – 301 BC), son of Philip from Elimeia, was a Macedonian Greek nobleman, general, satrap, and king. He was a major figure in the Wars of the Diadochi after Alexander's death, declaring himself king in 306 BC and establishing the Antigonid dynasty.

73 **Antagoras** of Rhodes (born on Rhodes about 270 B.C.) was a Greek poet. He was also noted for his cookery.

74 **Agamemnon** was a king of Mycenae, the son, or grandson, of King Atreus and Queen Aerope, the brother of Menelaus, the husband of Clytemnestra and the father of Iphigenia, Electra or Laodike, Orestes and Chrysothemis.

75 **Zeus and the Tortoise** (Aesop's Fable) - In the late 15th century, the Venetian Laurentius Abstemius created a Neo-Latin variant on the fable. It tells how, when the animals were invited to ask Zeus for gifts at the dawn of time, the snail asked if he could bring his house with him. Zeus asked if this would not be an annoying burden, but the snail replied that he preferred this way to avoid bad neighbors.

76 **Olympias** (Ancient Greek, c. 375–316 BC) was the eldest daughter of king Neoptolemus I of Epirus, the sister of Alexander I of Epirus, the fourth wife of Philip

II, the king of Macedonia and the mother of Alexander the Great.

[77] **Hecuba** (Ancient Greek) was a queen in Greek mythology, the wife of King Priam of Troy during the Trojan War, she had 19 children, who included major characters of Homer's Iliad such as the warriors Hector and Paris and the prophetess Cassandra. Two of them, Hector and Troilus are said to have been born as a result of Hecuba's relationship with the god Apollo.

[78] **Thetis** was a sea **nymph** who gave birth to the famous hero Achilles.

[79] **Cornelia**, (flourished 2nd century BC), highly cultured mother of the late 2nd-century BC Roman reformers Tiberius and Gaius. Sempronius Gracchus.

[80] *A Petite Pallace of Pettie his Pleasure*, licensed for the press to Richard Watkins on 6 August 1576, and was published soon afterwards.

[81] **The Temple of Dianae** had taken one-hundred twenty years to complete, with its destruction around 356 BC. On the night when Alexander the Great was said to have been born, the temple was deliberately burned down by Herostratus, who, setting fire to the wooden frame of the roof, hoped to immortalize his name. The Ephesians, however, decreed that his name never be recorded.

[82] **Freshwater Soldier** is a plant that lives on top of the water and has no roots.

[83] **Marcus Aurelius Antoninus** was a Roman emperor

from 161 to 180 and a Stoic philosopher.

[84] **Shrunk on their** necks – a euphemism during the late 16th century for a physical gesture showing obstinance, by pulling the chin toward the neck.

[85] In the 16th century, some scholars argued for the use of native terms over Latinate forms. Those who favored English branded what they considered ostentatious Latinisms "**inkhorn terms**" after the bottles carried by scholars, and since then we have used "**inkhorn**" as an adjective for pretentious language.

Printed in Great Britain
by Amazon

e78e5cb2-bdaf-4503-b5bd-592d243c9c77R01